the masala art

the masala art

INDIAN HAUTE CUISINE

Foreword
Vir Sanghvi

Lustre Press
Roli Books

ISBN: 978-81-7436-757-0

© Hemant Oberoi 2011
Published in India by Roli Books
in arrangement with Roli & Janssen BV
M-75, Greater Kailash II Market;
New Delhi-110 048, India.
Phone: ++91-11-29212271, 40682000
Fax: ++91-11-29217185
Email: info@rolibooks.com
Website: www.rolibooks.com

Editor: Neeta Datta
Design: Divya Bharadwaj, Bonita Vaz-Shimray
Prepress: Jyoti Dey

Printed and bound in Singapore

Contents

Author's Note

Life is so unpredictable. Never could I have imagined that I, who wanted to be a doctor or an army officer, would join the hotel industry to become a chef! But sometimes, there are people who come into our lives and suddenly turn them around. One such man was Mr A B Kerkar. He brought me to Bombay, the land of dreams, and gave me the chance to prove myself. I joined the Taj at the time of the great Chef Mascarenhas, whom we affectionately called Chef Masci. When I entered the culinary battlefield, hard work and no social life with, above all, a passion for creativity, were the keys to success. I learnt so much about life and food from that time.

I spent a lot of time creating new recipes and experimenting with classic and contemporary cuisines to create something beautiful. I feel anxious and exasperated when my ideas are hard to implement, but for me, cooking is like love. Once you are in a relationship with food, you either put your heart and soul into it or leave it altogether. I always tell my students that they should follow a few ground rules to be a good chef. I've had my share of people who are too preoccupied with getting to the top. Let me tell you something: there are no shortcuts. I did not get here just by putting in effort; I put

in the time. Listen to those above you; it takes time to grow up and learn from others. But at the same time, believe in yourself and your work. I've lived by these rules all my life and they have kept me grounded. Never leave the pan, or one day the pan will leave you!

Throughout my career, I have had the encouragement and support of two visionaries, Mr R K Krishna Kumar and Mr Tata, towards whom I would like to express my deepest gratitude.

Any team is like a pyramid where sometimes the leader is on top and sometimes one inverts it to take the load. I want to express my sincere appreciation to my team of dedicated chefs without whom nothing would be possible.

I owe a lot of my success to my family. My wife has tolerated my long hours and forgiven me for not devoting time to the family. She was the pillar of my strength when I needed it the most. After all the travels, I couldn't wait to come back home, craving basic nourishment, and would end up saying, '*Roti kithe hai?*' My two boys, even after seeing their dad slog it out all his life, chose to be a part of the Food & Beverage industry. They both work hard and I hope they find the same fulfillment as I do.

Masala Art is the culmination of my travels and experience in the global world of food. I have tried to incorporate timeless classics with modern cuisines to create something delightful to the palate. In India, we have varied cuisines, from food for the maharajas, to flavours from the humblest of fisher and village kitchens. The creation of Masala Art is the result of Indian cuisine being presented in a contemporary way without losing the flavour of the basic ingredients. It is all about devouring food with your eyes and palate.

Foreword

VIR SANGHVI

I've known Hemant Oberoi for over two decades now. When we first met, he was the newly appointed Executive Chef of the Taj Mahal Hotel in Bombay. I wondered then how Hemant would manage at the Taj, easily one of the world's greatest hotels but also, like many heritage hotels, set in its ways and resistant to change.

I needn't have worried. In a few years, Hemant had put his stamp so completely on the hotel's restaurants that it was hard to even think of the Taj without thinking of Hemant. He opened The Zodiac Grill and made it the finest French restaurant in India – and some would say, the best restaurant of any kind within its generation – with cuisine that was both surprising and vibrant.

Then, he took on the Taj's other restaurants, opening the Middle Eastern Souk, a product of his years working in the Gulf, in place of the old Apollo Bar; transforming and shifting The Shamiana and revamping the Golden Dragon, the restaurant that introduced Sichuan food to India.

By the end of the twentieth century, Hemant was India's best-known chef, recognized on the street, feted by the press and an inspiration to all young chefs. His responsibilities extended to include all of the Taj's luxury properties and he brought his touch to bear on restaurants all over India. His Wasabi (opened along with the Japanese Chef Masaharu Morimoto – though the menu is full of Hemant's dishes) has been rated as being among the world's 100 best restaurants for four years now. His Blue Ginger restaurants popularized Vietnamese food in Delhi and Bangalore.

But I guess he knew what the gap was. French chefs cook French food; Chinese chefs cook Chinese food and Indian chefs must cook Indian food.

Hotel chefs and corporate chefs are at a disadvantage in the sense that their own ambitions and aspirations must take second

Facing page: Chef Oberoi at his studio creating new dishes. *Above:* Chef Oberoi with the dignitaries-Bill Clinton, George Bush and Manmohan Singh.

9

The Three Grand Masters: Chef Oberoi with Jean George and Mr Nobu.

place to the priorities of their companies. And so, Hemant had little choice but to travel the world, looking for ingredients and dishes to reproduce in the kitchens of the Taj

But I knew, that in his heart, he longed to do an Indian restaurant on his own. The Taj had very successful Indian restaurants at all of its luxury properties – Tanjore in Bombay, Handi in Delhi etc. – but they were beginning to show their age. Hemant overhauled their menus, changed the chefs and added new dishes but he was always handicapped by having to tinker with somebody else's concept.

It wasn't till the Taj closed down the Handi in Delhi and asked Hemant to dream up a new restaurant to take its place, that Hemant finally had the opportunity he needed.

Indian restaurants at hotels have a (not entirely undeserved) bad reputation. Because the hotels cater to foreigners, chefs are urged to tone down the spice levels in their food so that they can offer tourists a safe and unthreatening dining experience. Tourists have heard of some of the famous dishes of Indian cuisine (tandoori chicken, vindaloo, chicken

tikka masala, etc.) and know these dishes in their bastardized versions. (In the case of chicken tikka masala the dish is as Indian as fish and chips; it was invented in England) so hotel managements pressure chefs to include some crowd-pleasers.

I knew that Hemant would eschew this formula. But what would he do instead? As India's best-known chef, he had his reputation to think of.

The vision he demonstrated in the planning of the new restaurant staggered me. Far from running away from spices, he embraced them. The restaurant would be called Masala Art, he said, and it would celebrate the wonders of Indian spices or masalas.

We Indians have always known that our cuisine is about spices. We love tandoori food but we regard Kabab restaurants as our versions of steak houses. Indian haute cuisine is about the interplay of spices and about the effects created by the masalas.

Having decided that he would focus on Indian haute cuisine, Hemant made another surprising decision. He would travel around the

Indian sub-continent and find dishes that rarely made it to restaurant menus (say, a fish curry from the Kerala town of Allepey or a chicken cooked with cocktail onions in the style of Lahore) and then finesse their spicing so that, by the time each dish was served, it would retain the authenticity of its provincial origins but would also suggest the sophistication of haute cuisine.

It was an interesting idea and I watched in amazement as Hemant dredged his memory for the dishes that his father, who worked for the railways and, therefore, travelled around India, had introduced his family to. Hemant went to railway stations in such cities as Amritsar and ate at *dhabhas* (or small, unpretentious restaurants) all over India looking for dishes where the spicing struck him as being unusual or noteworthy.

When Masala Art finally opened at Delhi's Taj Palace Hotel, it was like no other Indian restaurant. There were griddle *(tawa)* – cooking counters – derived from the *tawas* of roadside

cooking but, in this context, reminiscent of Japanese teppanyaki counters. Many of the dishes were cooked in olive oil and though purists believe that olive oil can interfere with the taste of spices, Hemant's ingenuity ensured that nothing tasted wrong.

Indian restaurants shirk from any of the robust ingredients that characterize traditional cooking. You'll rarely find sugarcane on a restaurant menu. But Hemant installed a sugarcane press in the restaurant and not only served fresh sugarcane juice but also made a sorbet out of it.

Indian chefs rarely serve *chapattis* in their restaurants even though few Indians ever eat restaurant-style *naans* and *tandoori rotis* at home. Hemant changed that. He insisted on a flour mill in the kitchen so that fresh wholewheat flour was ground before each meal. Then, the chef made your *chapattis* for you on a trolley in front of your table.

Hemant Oberoi with his team
in the World Gourmet
Summit at Las Vegas. He
was invited to showcase
Indian cuisine.

As you might imagine, Masala Art was a phenomenal success. Hemant quickly followed it up with two more Masala restaurants. He opened Masala Kraft (grander, with more emphasis on the forgotten great dishes of India) at the Taj Mahal Hotel and Masala Bay (more seafood) at the Taj Land's End, both in Bombay. Then came Masala Klub in Bangalore with a special section devoted to hot stone cooking.

Even as the Masala phenomenon was influencing restaurateurs all over India, Hemant came up with a second concept – a new and innovative school of Indian cuisine that merged international styles of presentation and cooking with Indian flavours. The first such restaurant, Varq opened in Delhi in 2009 (at the Taj Mahal – Masala Art is at the Taj Palace) and has been packed ever since. Later, Hemant took elements of this concept to London and Cape Town.

Rare is the Indian chef who can invent a successful cuisine concept on his own; rarer still is the chef who can do two different concepts and cook both simultaneously. But Hemant has pulled it off. He is now not just the best known chef in India, he is also the most influential Indian chef in the country.

Those of us who have known Hemant for years have always known of his love of Indian food. But because he has spent so long opening restaurants that specialized in other cuisines, the outside world sometimes lost sight of the fact that Indian food was Hemant's true passion.

I wonder sometimes: if Hemant had opened his Indian restaurants in 1990, when he first took over as the Taj's Chef, what would they have been like? My guess is that they would have been good but that there would have been no breakthroughs. The reason the Masala restaurants were so influential was because they were the creation of a chef at the height of his powers, of a man who had seen it all and done it all.

Hemant is in a competitive business. So I wondered if he would be ready to share his ultimate resource: his recipe. Any halfway decent chef can make *gucchi khumb* or *macchi chutneywali*. The reason the Masala restaurants work is because Hemant has put a subtle spin on each dish. So would he be willing to part with those secrets?

I am pleased to see that he is willing to share his recipes. Most recipe books by celebrity chefs either simplify the food so much that you wonder what the fuss was about or they offer only part of each recipe.

This book is unusual because it is the real thing. Cook these recipes and you will make the Masala Art / Bay / Kraft originals. There is no artifice here – just a chef parting with his secrets.

That alone makes this book unusual. But what makes it really special is that it is the first book by India's best-known chef; that it is not an ego trip by some TV chef; and that these are the recipes to the dishes that make India's best restaurants so successful. Like the restaurants, the book is a breakthrough.

A Day in the Life of ...

Hemant Oberoi's office is in the heart of his domain - the kitchen of Taj Mahal Hotel in Mumbai. The clanging of pots and pans blends with the aroma of spices and simmering food while chefs dash around putting together the assorted menus for the day. Inside the office hangs a plaque which reads: 'Never, but never, question the Chef's judgement.' The finality of the words is as emphatic as the credentials of the man displaying them.

Hemant Oberoi has been with the Taj for 27 years. 15 of them as executive chef. That's a long time to have worked in one place, but Oberoi still sees each day as a new challenge, and a chance to show off his culinary skills.

Chef Hemant Oberoi with his core team pose for a photo shoot with Gateway of India in the background

7:00am Hemant Oberoi likes to wake up early whenever possible to take a 3.8 km walk on Mumbai's beautiful Marine Drive.

9:00am Oberoi has his first cup of tea and scours the paper in his office that's adorned with awards. Oberoi's award-winning Wasabi by Morimoto at The Taj Mahal Palace appeared on the 54th position in the top 100 restaurants of the world's list by S. Pellegrino.

9:30am 'My first task is to go through all the restaurant log books,' says Oberoi, who examines each one in detail to understand the recorded number of covers and business generated at all the restaurants.

11:00am Oberoi joins his colleagues for breakfast. This is the first meal of the day and Oberoi briefs his men on various things: checking the sizes of papayas, controlling costs, GSTS or Guest Satisfaction Tracking System and so on. After this he sits down to enjoy two egg white omelettes.

12:00pm Checking the menus for the next day or two, Oberoi plays particular attention to banquet and VIP functions. 'I always try and be around to greet VIPs as far as possible,' he says.

1:00pm Oberoi walks through the hotel conducting surprise checks at Golden Dragon and Shamiana. He checks the quality of the fish at the various restaurants. 'We only buy raw material. No cooked food will come to this hotel. That's our policy.'

3:00pm Oberoi finally sits down for lunch and eats the staff dining room food along with some stir-fried fish from Golden Dragon. 'I love fish,' he says. 'Fish and vegetables - they are my staple.'

4:00pm Back in his office, Oberoi speaks to all the head chefs to discuss a formal banquet.

5:00pm Oberoi send his sous chef Ramu to plan a Mumbai socialite's party

7:00pm Oberoi is apprised of the evening bookings and receives and SMS letting him know if any known VIP is coming to his restaurants. Oberoi then walks through the recently restored hotel, meeting and greeting guests.

11:00pm Dinner time. Oberoi orders the chargrilled salmon from Masala Kraft.

11:30pm He finally packs up for the day. 'My only meal at home is tea. Every night, I have a cup of tea as soon as I get home.'

soups and beverages

Beetroot Lassi

Beetroot flavoured yoghurt drink

INGREDIENTS

2 cups / 400 ml / 14 fl oz Beetroot (*chukandar*)
  juice
2 cups / 400 gm / 14 oz Yoghurt (*dahi*)
1 cup / 200 gm / 7 oz Sugar

METHOD

1. Whisk yoghurt with sugar and add beetroot juice.

2. Serve chilled.

Ananas Panna

Refreshing pineapple drink

INGREDIENTS

1 Pineapple (*ananas*), unripened, medium-sized,
  cut into small pieces
½ cup / 100 gm / 3½ oz Sugar
½ tsp / 2½ gm Black salt (*kala namak*)
¼ tsp Cardamom (*elaichi*) powder
10 Mint (*pudina*) leaves, fresh, shredded

METHOD

1. Boil the pineapple with 1 cup water along
   with sugar, black salt, cardamom powder,
   and mint leaves.
2. Blend the mix to a fine paste, add 4 cups /
   800 ml of water and serve chilled.

Bhune Makai ka Shorba

Roasted corn soup

INGREDIENTS

4 Corn on the cob, roasted
Or
2½ cups / 500 gm / 1.1 lb Corn kernels, dry
2 tbsp / 30 ml / 1 fl oz Vegetable oil
2 Bay leaves (tej patta)
4 Green cardamoms (choti elaichi)
½ cup / 100 gm / 3½ oz Onions, sliced
1 tbsp / 15 gm Ginger (adrak)
1 tsp / 5 gm Green chillies
½ cup / 100 gm / 3½ oz Carrots (gajar),
  sliced
2 (1 x 4) Tomatoes
1 tsp / 5 gm Madras curry powder
½ tsp / 2½ gm Turmeric (haldi) powder
¼ cup / 50 gm / 1¾ oz Roasted Bengal gram
  (chana dal) powder
Salt to taste
¼ bunch Mint (pudina) leaves
¼ bunch Green coriander (hara dhaniya)
  roots
½ cup / 100 gm / 3½ oz Popcorns

METHOD

1. Heat the oil and fry the bay leaves and green cardamoms. Sauté the onions, ginger, green chillies, carrots, tomatoes, Madras curry powder, and turmeric powder.
2. Add roasted corn kernels followed by Bengal gram powder. Add 4 cups / 800 ml of water and salt and bring to the boil.
3. Add mint leaves and green coriander roots; simmer for half an hour. Then blend to a fine soup. If required strain the soup
4. Boil the soup and season. Serve hot garnished with popcorns

23

Hare Chane ka Shorba

Green gram soup

INGREDIENTS

2 cups / 400 gm / 14 oz Green gram (*hara chana*), boiled
2 tbsp / 30 ml / 1 fl oz Vegetable oil
2 Bay leaves (*tej patta*)
4 Green cardamoms (*choti elaichi*)
½ cup / 100 gm / 3½ oz Onions, sliced
1 tbsp / 15 gm Ginger (*adrak*)
1 tsp / 5 gm Green chillies
½ cup / 100 gm / 3½ oz Carrots (*gajar*), sliced
2 (1 x 4) Tomatoes
1 tsp / 5 gm Madras curry powder
½ tsp / 2½ gm Turmeric (*haldi*) powder
¼ cup / 50 gm / 1¾ oz Roasted Bengal gram (*chana dal*) powder
Salt to taste
¼ bunch Mint (*pudina*) leaves
¼ bunch Green coriander (*hara dhaniya*) roots

METHOD

1. Heat the oil and fry the bay leaves and green cardamoms. Sauté the onions, ginger, green chillies, carrots, tomatoes, Madras curry powder, and turmeric powder.
2. Add green gram followed by Bengal gram powder. Add 4 cups / 800 ml water and salt and bring to the boil.
3. Add mint leaves and green coriander roots and simmer for half an hour. Then blend to a fine soup. If required strain the soup.
4. Boil the soup and season. Serve hot garnished with mint leaves.

Lemon Grass Rasam

Tomato soup flavoured with lemon grass

INGREDIENTS

For the lentil broth
4 (1 x 4) Tomatoes
1 cup / 200 gm / 7 oz Pigeon peas (*toover dal*)
4 sticks Lemon grass, fresh
2 Kafir lime leaves, shredded
2 Garlic (*lasan*) pods
8 Black peppercorns (*sabut kali mirch*)
1 tbsp / 15 gm Coriander (*dhaniya*) seeds
¼ tsp Cumin (*jeera*) seeds
4 seeds Tamarind (*imli*), soaked in warm
 water
1 tbsp / 15 gm *Rasam powder*
Salt to taste

For the tempering
1 tbsp / 15 ml Vegetable oil
¼ tsp Mustard seeds (*rai*)
¼ tsp Asafoetida (*hing*)
6 Cherry chillies, dried
8 Curry leaves (*kadhi patta*)

METHOD

1. **For the lentil broth**, make the broth with tomatoes, pigeon peas, lemon grass and kafir lime leaves.
2. To the simmering broth add garlic, black peppercorns, coriander seeds, and cumin seeds (all crushed together).
3. Add tamarind extract, *rasam powder* and salt. Strain the lemon grass and lentil broth.
4. **For the tempering**, heat the oil; sauté the mustard seeds, asafoetida, cherry chillies, and curry leaves and pour into the lemon grass rasam. Serve hot.

fish and seafood

Achari Lobster

Pickled lobsters

INGREDIENTS

4 Jumbo lobsters, whole with tail,
 cleaned
2 tbsp / 30 ml / 1 fl oz Lemon (*nimbu*) juice
½ tsp / 2½ gm Turmeric (*haldi*) powder
1 tsp / 5 gm Red chilli powder
1 tbsp / 15 ml Mustard (*sarson*) oil
2 tbsp / 30 gm / 1 oz Pickle paste (available in
 Indian grocery stores)
1 tsp / 5 gm Ginger-garlic (*adrak-lasan*) paste
¼ cup / 50 gm / 1¾ oz Yoghurt (*dahi*)
½ tsp / 2½ gm Fennel (*saunf*) powder
¼ tsp *Chaat masala*
½ tsp / 2½ gm Onion seeds (*kalonji*)
1 tbsp / 15 gm Butter for basting

For the presentation
4 Lobster heads, trimmed, blanched
4 Lobster shells, blanched

METHOD

1. Marinate the lobsters with lemon juice.
    Drain the excess liquid after 2 minutes.
2. Add turmeric powder, red chilli powder,
    mustard oil, pickle paste, ginger-garlic
    paste, yoghurt, and fennel powder to the
    lobster. Retain for 15 minutes.
3. Cook the lobster in the tandoor on a
    skewer basting with butter. Sprinkle *chaat
    masala* and onion seeds on the lobster and
    serve in the shell with head presented on
    the side.

Alleppey Meen Curry

Fish in coconut curry

INGREDIENTS

12 Fish darnes (Seer / Pomfret)
2 tbsp / 30 ml / 1 fl oz Coconut (*nariyal*) oil
1 tsp / 5 gm Mustard seeds (*rai*)
8 Shallots (Madras onions), sliced
1 tbsp / 15 gm Ginger (*adrak*), julienned
4 Green chillies, slit
12 Curry leaves (*kadhi patta*)
¾ tsp / 3¾ gm Turmeric (*haldi*) powder
1 tsp / 5 gm Red chilli powder
1 Raw mango, peeled, cut into wedges
2 cups / 400 gm / 14 oz Coconut paste, fine
Salt to taste

METHOD

1. Heat the oil and fry the mustard seeds. Add shallots, ginger, green chillies, and curry leaves.
2. Add turmeric powder and red chilli powder. Add raw mango, coconut paste, fish, and salt. Add 3 cups / 600 ml water.
3. Simmer the fish in the coconut curry till it is cooked. Serve hot with steamed rice.

Anardana Jheenga

Prawns flavoured with pomegranate

INGREDIENTS

For the marinade
28 / 21-25 kg Prawns without tail
½ tsp / 2½ gm Turmeric (*haldi*) powder
Salt to taste
1 Juice of lemon (*nimbu*)
1 tbsp / 15 gm Ginger-garlic (*adrak-lasan*) paste

For the masala
¼ cup / 50 ml / 1¾ fl oz Vegetable oil
1 tsp / 5 gm Garlic (*lasan*), chopped
1 tsp / 5 gm Coriander (*dhaniya*) seeds and
  chillies, crushed
1 tsp / 5 gm Ginger (*adrak*), chopped
1 Green chilli, chopped
1 tsp / 5 gm Red chilli powder
1 tbsp / 15 gm Red chilli paste
2 cups / 400 gm / 14 oz Tomatoes, chopped
Salt to taste

For tossing
1 tbsp / 15 ml Vegetable oil
1 tsp / 5 gm Cumin (*jeera*) seeds
1 tsp / 5 gm Garlic, chopped
1 tsp / 5 gm Ginger, chopped
1 Green chilli, chopped
3 Bell peppers (*Shimla mirch*), diced into
  1" squares
a pinch Dried fenugreek powder (*kasoori
  methi*)
1 tsp / 5 gm *Chaat masala*
½ cup / 100 gm / 3½ oz Pomegranate seeds
  (*anar dana*), fresh
a pinch *Garam masala* powder
1 Juice of lemon

METHOD

1. **For the marinade**, marinate the prawns with turmeric powder, salt, lemon juice, and ginger-garlic paste.
2. **For the masala**, heat the oil and sauté the garlic. Add crushed coriander and chilli.
3. Add ginger, green chilli, red chilli powder, and chilli paste. Add tomatoes and cook for 8 -10 minutes.
4. Add salt and remove from heat. Cool and retain the masala.
5. **For tossing**, heat the oil and fry the cumin seeds, garlic, ginger, green chilli, and bell peppers.
6. Add the prawns followed by the tomato masala and cook over moderate heat.
7. Add dried fenugreek powder, *chaat masala*, pomegranate seeds, *garam masala* powder, and lemon juice to finish.

Bhatti ka Jheenga

Chargrilled prawns

INGREDIENTS

12 Jumbo prawns with tail, deveined

For the marinade
2 tbsp / 30 ml / 1 fl oz Lemon (*nimbu*) juice
1 tbsp / 15 gm *Bhatti masala* (see note)
½ cup / 100 gm / 3½ oz Yoghurt (*dahi*), thick
½ tsp / 2½ gm Red chilli powder
½ tsp / 2½ gm Coriander (*dhaniya*) powder
1 tbsp / 15 gm Ginger-garlic (*adrak-lasan*) paste
2 tbsp / 30 ml / 1 fl oz Vegetable oil
Salt to taste

For the presentation
1 tsp / 5 gm *Chaat masala*
4 Lemon, cut into wedges
4 Pineapple (*ananas*) slices

METHOD

1. Wash and marinate the prawns with all the ingredients mentioned and reserve for 20 minutes.
2. Chargrill the prawns till cooked. Sprinkle *chaat masala* and serve hot with lemon wedges and grilled pineapple slices.

Note: *To make* bhatti masala: *mix equal proportions of coriander seeds, black salt, cumin powder, red chilli powder, and crushed black peppercorns.*

Crab Galouti

Pan-fried crab cakes

INGREDIENTS

2 cups / 400 gm / 14 oz Raw crab meat
1 tsp / 5 gm Onion, golden, crushed
1 tsp / 5 gm Fried curry leaves (*kadhi patta*), powdered
½ tsp / 2½ gm Madras curry powder
1 tsp / 5 gm Ginger-garlic (*adrak-lasan*) paste
1 tbsp / 15 ml Coconut (*nariyal*) milk powder
Salt to taste
¼ tsp Black pepper (*kali mirch*) powder
½ tsp / 2½ gm Fennel (*saunf*) powder
¼ tsp Turmeric (*haldi*) powder
2 tbsp / 30 gm / 1 oz Butter / Ghee
2 tbsp / 30 gm / 1 oz Roasted gram flour (*besan*) powder
½ tsp / 2½ gm Yellow chilli powder

METHOD

1. Blend the crab meat to a fine paste and rub in all the ingredients.
2. Divide the mixture equally into small portions and shape into patties with wet palm. Pan-fry the patties in moderately hot oil till evenly brown. Remove and drain the excess oil on absorbent kitchen towels.
3. Serve hot with onion rings and lemon wedges.

Crab Samosas

Deep-fried crab triangles

INGREDIENTS

For the dough
2 cups / 400 gm / 14 oz Refined flour (*maida*)
½ cup / 100 ml / 3½ fl oz Vegetable oil
Salt to taste

For the stuffing
250 gm / 8 oz Crab meat
1 tbsp / 15 ml Vegetable oil
1 tsp / 5 gm Garlic (*lasan*), chopped
1 tsp / 5 gm Ginger (*adrak*), chopped
1 tbsp / 15 gm Shallots, chopped
8 Curry leaves (*kadhi patta*), shredded
1 tsp / 5 gm Madras curry powder
½ tsp / 2¼ gm Dry red chillies (*sookhi lal mirch*),
   crushed
1 tbsp / 15 ml Coconut (*nariyal*) milk powder
Salt to taste
a pinch Fennel (*saunf*) powder
½ tsp / 2½ gm Black pepper (*kali mirch*)
   powder

For frying
4 cups / 800 ml / 28 fl oz Vegetable oil

METHOD

1. **For the dough**, make a semi-hard dough using flour, oil, salt and water as required. Rest the dough for 1 hour covered with a wet cloth.
2. **For the stuffing**, heat the oil; add garlic, ginger, and shallots; sauté.
3. Add curry leaves, Madras curry powder, crushed chillies, and crab meat. Cook for 5 minutes or till the mixture is dry.
4. Finish the mixture with coconut milk powder, salt, fennel powder, and black pepper powder. Keep aside to cool.
5. Divide the dough into small balls and roll each into a round sheet of 2 mm thickness.
6. Cut the sheet into half, stuff it with the mixture and shape into a triangle like a *samosa*.
7. Heat the oil in a wok (*kadhai*); fry the *samosas*, in medium-hot oil, till golden brown. Remove with a slotted spoon and drain the excess oil on absorbent kitchen towels.
8. Serve hot with tamarind chutney.

Crab Varqui

Layered peppered crab served with prawns

INGREDIENTS

For the peppered crab
250 gm / 8 oz Crab meat
1 tbsp / 15 ml Vegetable oil
1 tsp / 5 gm Garlic (*lasan*), chopped
1 tsp / 5 gm Ginger (*adrak*), chopped
2 tbsp / 30 gm / 1 oz Onions, chopped
1 Green chilli, chopped
8 Curry leaves (*kadhi patta*), shredded
10 Black peppercorns (*sabut kali mirch*),
  crushed
Salt to taste
½ tsp / 2½ gm Fennel (*saunf*) seed, powder
a pinch Turmeric (*haldi*) powder
1 tsp / 5 gm Madras curry powder
2 tbsp / 30 ml / 1 fl oz Coconut (*nariyal*) milk
  powder
a pinch *Garam masala* powder

For the prawns
4 Prawns with tail (U21-25)
Salt to taste
1 Lemon (*nimbu*)
½ tsp / 2½ gm Red chilli powder
1 tbsp / 15 ml Red chilli paste
2 tbsp / 30 gm / 1 oz Yoghurt (*dahi*), hung
1 tsp / 5 ml Mustard (*sarson*) oil
a pinch *Garam masala* powder
1 tsp / 5 gm Ginger-garlic paste
1 tbsp / 15 ml Vegetable oil

For the presentation
4 Red chilli flowers, fresh
8 Chives
15 Baked filo pastry sheets

METHOD

1. **For the peppered crab**, heat the oil; add garlic, ginger, onions, green chilli, curry leaves black pepper powder, fennel powder, turmeric powder, and Madras curry powder.; sauté for a while. Add crab meat and cook.
2. Add coconut milk powder and *garam masala* powder; mix well.
3. **For the prawns**, apply salt and lemon juice to the prawns.
4. Marinate the prawns in a mixture of red chilli powder, red chilli paste, salt, yoghurt, mustard oil, *garam masala* powder, and ginger-garlic paste.
5. Cook the prawns with tail up.
6. Interlayer the filo sheets with crab meat and finish with prawns on the top layer. Serve garnished with red chilli flowers and chives.

Mahi Tukra in Potato Baskets

Spiced fish cubes in potato baskets

INGREDIENTS

For the marinade
40 Fish cubes (1.5"), washed
Salt to taste
2 Juice of lemons (*nimbu*)
1 cup / 200 gm / 7 oz Gram flour (*besan*)
1 tbsp / 15 gm Refined flour (*maida*)
1 tsp / 5 gm Red chilli powder
1 Egg
1 tbsp / 15 gm Red chilli paste
1 tsp / 5 gm Ginger-garlic (*adrak-lasan*) paste
½ tsp / 2½ gm Bishop's weed (*ajwain*)
Vegetable oil for frying

For the tempering
1 tbsp / 15 ml Vegetable oil
2 pods Garlic (*lasan*), chopped
1 tbsp / 15 gm Green chillies, chopped
1 tbsp / 15 gm Ginger, chopped
1 Green pepper (*Shimla mirch*), diced into 1.5"
   pieces
1 Red pepper, diced into 1.5" pieces
1 Yellow pepper, diced into 1.5" pieces
1 Tomato, diced into 1.5" pieces
1 Onion, diced into 1.5" pieces
½ tsp / 2½ gm Red chilli powder
1 tsp / 5 gm Cumin (*jeera*) powder
1 tsp / 5 gm Chaat masala
1 Juice of lemon (*nimbu*)
½ cup / 100 gm / 3½ oz Green coriander (*hara
   dhaniya*), chopped
4 Potato baskets for presentation (see note)

METHOD

1. **For the marinade**, marinate the fish cubes with salt, lemon juice, gram flour, refined flour, red chilli powder, egg, chilli paste, ginger garlic paste, and Bishop's weed.
2. Lightly fry the fish cubes in hot oil till golden brown.
3. **For the tempering**, heat the oil in a pan; add garlic and fry. Add green chillies, ginger, bell peppers, tomato, and onion.
4. Now add the pre-fried fish cubes. Season with red chilli powder, cumin powder, and *chaat masala*.
5. Toss everything together. Sprinkle lemon juice and garnish with green coriander.
6. Serve in potato baskets.

Note: *For the potato baskets, peel and grate 500 gm / 1.1 lb potatoes with a madeline grater and soak in salted water. Drain the water and put the potatoes in a double tea strainer and fry in hot oil till crisp. Use as required*

Fish in Vine Leaves

Spiced fish wrapped in vine leaves

INGREDIENTS

8 / 120 gm / 4 oz Pomfret / Hamachi fillet
8 Vine leaves, big, cleaned, blanched
2 tbsp / 30 ml / 1 fl oz Lemon (*nimbu*) juice
Salt to taste
2 tbsp / 30 ml / 1 fl oz Vegetable oil
1 cup / 200 gm / 7 oz Shallots (Madras onion),
    chopped
1 tsp / 5 gm Garlic (*lasan*), chopped
1 tsp / 5 gm Ginger (*adrak*), chopped
½ tsp / 2½ gm Turmeric (*haldi*) powder
1 tsp / 5 gm Coriander (*dhaniya*) powder
1 tsp / 5 gm Red chilli powder
15 Curry leaves (*kadhi patta*), shredded
1 cup / 200 gm / 7 oz Tomatoes, chopped
Salt to taste
1 tsp / 5 gm Black peppercorns (*sabut kali
    mirch*), crushed
1 tbsp / 15 ml White wine vinegar (*sirka*)
2 tbsp / 30 ml / 1 fl oz Vegetable oil for cooking

METHOD

1. Apply salt and lemon juice to the fish fillets
    and rest for 5 minutes.
2. Heat the oil in a pan; fry the shallots,
    garlic, ginger, turmeric powder, coriander
    powder, red chilli powder, curry leaves, and
    tomatoes.
3. Cook till the oil separates from the masala.
    Season with salt, pepper, and white wine
    vinegar. Cool the mixture.
4. Apply the above masala equally to all
    fillets and wrap them in vine leaves.
5. Heat the oil in a pan; sear the wrapped fish
    and cook in a covered pan for 8 minutes.
6. Serve hot garnished with lemon slices.

Hare Pyaz ka Jheenga

Prawns cooked with spring onions

INGREDIENTS

32 Prawns (U21-25), deveined
¼ cup / 50 ml / 1¾ fl oz Vegetable oil
1 tsp / 5 gm Cumin (*jeera*) seeds
1 tbsp / 15 gm Garlic (*lasan*), chopped
1 tbsp / 15 gm Ginger (*adrak*), chopped
1 tsp / 5 gm Green chillies, chopped
½ tsp / 2½ gm Turmeric (*haldi*) powder
1 cup / 200 gm / 7 oz Spring onions (*hara pyaz*)
    white, sliced
2 cups / 400 gm / 14 oz Spinach (*palak*) purée
2 cups / 400 gm / 14 oz Spring onion greens,
    chopped
1 tsp / 5 gm Fenugreek powder (*kasoori methi*)
1 tbsp / 15 gm Butter
2 (1 x 4) Tomatoes, quarters
Salt to taste

METHOD

1. Heat the oil in a pan; fry the cumin seeds,
    garlic, ginger, and green chillies. Add
    turmeric powder and sauté the onion
    whites.
2. Add prawns and sauté. Add salt and
    spinach purée. Cook on low heat, partly
    covered, for 10 minutes.
3. Add onion greens and fenugreek powder.
    Finish with butter and serve hot garnished
    with tomato quarters.

Karwari Prawns

Deep-fried prawns served with coconut chutney

INGREDIENTS

For the prawns
24 Prawns with tail (U21-25), cleaned, washed
2 tbsp / 30 ml / 1 fl oz Lemon (*nimbu*) juice
1 tbsp / 15 gm Ginger-garlic (*adrak-lasan*)
  paste
1 tsp / 5 gm Red chilli powder
1 tbsp / 15 gm Red chilli paste
1 tsp / 5 gm Cumin (*jeera*) powder
1 tsp / 5 gm Turmeric (*haldi*) powder
1 Egg
½ cup / 100 / 3½ oz Tamarind (*imli*), soaked
2 cups / 400 gm / 14 oz Semolina (*sooji*)
Salt to taste
Vegetable oil for frying

For the chutney
1 cup / 200 gm / 7 oz Coconut (*nariyal*), fresh,
  grated
4 Dry Kashmiri chillies (*sookhi lal mirch*)
4 Dry red chillies, button
a pinch Asafoetida (*hing*)
6 Curry leaves (*kadhi patta*)
1 tbsp / 15 ml Vegetable oil for tempering

METHOD

1. **For the prawns**, apply salt, lemon juice
    and ginger-garlic paste on the prawns.
    Rest for 5 minutes.
2. Drain excess water, and add red chilli
    powder, red chilli paste, cumin powder,
    turmeric powder, egg and tamarind
    extract; mix well.
3. Coat the prawns with semolina and press
    between palms. Deep-fry in moderately
    hot oil and serve hot with coconut chutney.
4. **For the chutney**, make a fine paste of
    grated coconut and Kashmiri chillies and
    temper with button chillies, asafoetida and
    curry leaves.

Lobster Hawa Mahal

Lobster meat interlayered with spinach and saffron rice

INGREDIENTS

1 kg / 2.2 lb Lobster meat, cut into 2" cubes, washed
4 Lobster shells, washed, cut lengthwise into half
1 tsp / 5 ml Lemon (*nimbu*) juice
Salt to taste

For the egg batter
4 Eggs
Salt to taste
¼ tsp Turmeric (*haldi*) powder
1 tbsp / 15 gm Green coriander (*hara dhaniya*), chopped

For the masala
½ cup / 100 ml / 3½ fl oz Vegetable oil
1 tsp / 5 gm Cumin (*jeera*) seeds
1 cup / 200 gm / 7 oz Onions, chopped
1 tbsp / 15 gm Ginger-garlic (*adrak-lasan*) paste
½ tsp / 2½ gm Turmeric (*haldi*) powder
1 tsp / 5 gm Red chilli powder
1 cup / 200 gm / 7 oz Tomatoes, chopped
Salt to taste

For the spinach
1 cup / 200 gm / 7 oz Spinach (*palak*)
¼ tsp Cumin seeds
1 tsp / 5 gm Garlic, chopped
½ cup / 100 gm / 3½ oz Onions, chopped

METHOD

1. Mix salt and lemon juice with the lobster meat and keep aside for 10 minutes.
2. Blanch the lobster shells and retain.
3. **For the egg batter**, whisk the eggs in a bowl with salt, turmeric powder, and green coriander.
4. **For the masala**, heat the oil in a pan and fry the cumin seeds. Add onions and fry till light golden in colour.
5. Fry ginger garlic paste, add turmeric powder, and red chilli powder. Add tomatoes and salt; cook the masala till it starts to leave oil.
6. Sear the lobster in a hot pan and cook with the above masala using a little water.
7. **For the spinach**, sauté the spinach with cumin seeds, garlic and onions. Keep aside.
8. Interlayer saffron rice, spinach and lobster mixture. Pour the egg mixture over it and bake till golden brown.

Masala Sea Bass

Sea bass served on a bed of spinach and mushrooms

INGREDIENTS

For the sea bass
4 / 180 gm / 6 oz Chilean sea bass
Salt to taste
1 tbsp / 15 ml Lemon (*nimbu*) juice
½ tsp / 2½ gm Ginger-garlic (*adrak-lasan*) paste
½ tsp / 2½ gm Turmeric (*haldi*) powder
2 tbsp / 30 ml / 1 fl oz Vegetable oil

For the mushroom mix
1 cup / 200 gm / 7 oz Mushrooms, button,
   washed, pat dried, cut into 4 pieces each
2 Shitake
6 Hon shimeji
6 Chanterelles
1 tbsp / 15 ml Vegetable oil
½ tsp / 2½ gm Garlic, chopped
1 tbsp / 15 gm Onions, chopped
Salt to taste

For the spinach
1 cup / 200 gm / 7 oz Spinach (*palak*) purée
1 tbsp / 15 ml Vegetable oil
1 tbsp / 15 gm Onion, chopped
½ tsp / 2½ gm Garlic, chopped
1 tsp / 5 gm Ginger, chopped
½ tsp / 2½ gm Green chillies, chopped
¼ tsp Turmeric powder
1 tsp / 5 gm Butter

¼ tsp Fenugreek powder (*kasoori methi*)
Salt to taste

For the presentation
4 Chive tips
4 Red chilli flowers
2 tbsp / 30 ml / 1 fl oz Chilli oil
4 Lemons, cut into wedges

METHOD

1. **For the sea bass**, marinate the sea bass in
   salt, lemon juice, ginger-garlic paste, and
   turmeric powder for 20 minutes.
2. Heat the oil in a pan; sear the fish and
   cook at 180°C / 350°F for 12 minutes.
3. **For the mushrooms**, heat the oil in a
   pan and fry the garlic and onions. Add
   mushrooms and salt and cook till moisture
   dries from the mushrooms.
4. **For the spinach**, heat the oil in a pan. Fry
   the onion, garlic, ginger, and green chillies.
   Add turmeric powder, spinach, and salt.
5. Cook the spinach for 5 minutes. Add
   butter and fenugreek powder.
6. Present the cooked sea bass on a bed of
   spinach and mushrooms garnished with
   chive tips, lemon wedges, chilli flowers
   and oil.

Patrani Macchi

Coconut fish steamed in banana leaves

INGREDIENTS

8 / 120 gm / 4 oz Fish fillets, cleaned, washed
1 tbsp / 15 ml Vinegar (*sirka*)
Salt to taste
2 Banana leaves to wrap each fillet, trimmed, washed
¼ cup / 50 ml / 1¾ fl oz Vegetable oil
20 Curry leaves (*kadhi patta*)
2 Lemons (*nimbu*), cut into wedges

For the coconut chutney
1 cup / 200 gm / 7 oz Coconut (*nariyal*), fresh, cut into pieces
1 cup / 200 gm / 7 oz Green coriander (*hara dhaniya*), chopped
4 Green chillies, washed, slit, seeds removed
4 pods Garlic (*lasan*), peeled
1 small piece Ginger (*adrak*), chopped
1 tsp / 5 gm Red chilli powder
1 tbsp / 15 gm Coriander (*dhaniya*) seeds
1 tsp / 5 gm Cumin (*jeera*) seeds
2 Lemon juice
1 tbsp / 15 gm Sugar
Salt to taste

METHOD

1. Make horizontal slits on the fish pieces. Sprinkle vinegar and salt and marinate for 30 minutes.
2. **For the coconut chutney**, put all the ingredients mentioned in a grinder to make a smooth paste. Keep aside.
3. Marinate the fish pieces with the coconut chutney and spread the rest on both sides. Apply oil on banana leaves and wrap each piece separately.
4. Steam the wrapped fish pieces for 15 minutes.
5. Then remove the fish from steam, unwrap and arrange on a platter. Serve with lemon wedges.

Macchi Chutneywali

Deep-fried minty fish

INGREDIENTS

4 Pomfret fillets
1 tbsp / 15 ml Lemon (*nimbu*) juice
Salt to taste
½ cup / 100 gm / 3½ oz Gram flour (*besan*)
1 tbsp / 15 gm Refined flour (*maida*)
1 Egg, beaten
Tooth picks
Vegetable oil for frying

For the mint chutney
1 cup / 200 gm / 7 oz Mint (*pudina*) leaves
½ cup / 100 gm / 3½ oz Green coriander
  (*hara dhaniya*)
2 Green chillies
½ Raw mango, medium-sized
1 tsp / 5 gm Ginger (*adrak*), chopped
Salt to taste

For the presentation
1 tsp / 5 gm *Chaat masala*
4 Lemon, cut into wedges
½ cup / 100 gm / 3½ oz Onion rings
½ cup / 100 gm / 3½ oz Carrot (*gajar*) curls
½ cup / 100 gm / 3½ oz Beetroot (*chukundar*)
  curls

METHOD

1. **For the mint chutney**, blend all the
   ingredients of the chutney to a fine paste.
2. Marinate the fillets in salt and lemon juice
   for 5 minutes.
3. Apply chutney on the fish and coat the
   fish with gram flour, refined flour, and egg
   batter. Shape into a cone with the help of a
   tooth pick.
4. Deep-fry in oil till the fish is cooked and
   crisp from the outside. Sprinkle *chaat
   masala*, garnish with onion rings, carrot
   and beetroot curls and serve hot with
   acompaniments.

Prawn Idiappam Rolls

Steam prawns wrapped with string hopper rolls

INGREDIENTS

For the prawn mix
50 / 1 kg / 2.2 lb Prawns
2 tbsp / 30 ml / 1 fl oz Vegetable oil
½ tsp / 2½ gm Mustard seeds (*rai*)
8 Curry leaves (*kadhi patta*), shredded
1 tsp / 5 gm Garlic (*lasan*), chopped
2 tsp / 10 gm Ginger (*adrak*), chopped
½ cup / 100 gm / 3½ oz Onions, chopped
½ cup / 100 gm / 3½ oz Tomatoes, chopped
½ tsp / 2½ gm Red chilli powder
Salt to taste
2 tbsp / 30 ml / 1 fl oz Coconut (*nariyal*) milk
   powder
1 tsp / 5 ml Lemon (*nimbu*) juice

For the string hopper (*idiappam*) rolls
3 cups / 600 gm / 22 oz Rice flour
1 tbsp / 15 ml Coconut (*nariyal*) oil
2 cups / 400 ml / 14 fl oz Hot water

METHOD

1. **For the prawn mix**, heat the oil in a wok (*kadhai*); add mustard seeds, curry leaves, garlic, ginger, onions, tomatoes, and red chilli powder. Cook till the oil separates.
2. Add prawns, salt, coconut milk powder and lemon juice.
3. **For the string hopper (*idiappam*) rolls,** make hot water dough using rice flour, salt, and coconut oil.
4. Roll the prawn mix in rice flour mixture, wrap and steam for 8 minutes at 110°C / 230°F.
5. Serve hot with tomato kut (see recipe on p. 57).

Prawn Kuzhambu

Prawns cooked in tangy tomato curry

INGREDIENTS

32 Prawns (U21-25), deveined
3 cups / 600 gm / 22 oz Tomatoes, chopped
½ cup / 100 gm / 3½ oz Coconut (*nariyal*),
    grated
2 tbsp / 30 ml / 1 fl oz Vegetable oil
½ tsp / 2½ gm Mustard seeds (*rai*)
1 tsp / 5 gm Black gram (*urad dal*), split
½ tsp / 2½ gm Cumin (*jeera*) seeds
½ tsp / 2½ gm Fenugreek seeds (*methi dana*)
15 Curry leaves (*kadhi patta*)
2 Green chillies, slit
1 tsp / 5 gm Red chilli powder
½ tsp / 2½ gm Turmeric (*haldi*) powder
1 tsp / 5 gm Coriander (*dhaniya*) powder
Salt to taste
15 Shallots (Madras onions), peeled, whole
4 seeds Tamarind (*imli*), soaked

METHOD

1. Blend the coconut and tomatoes to a fine paste.
2. Heat the oil in a pan; fry the mustard seeds, black gram, cumin seeds, and fenugreek seeds. Add curry leaves, green chillies, red chilli powder, turmeric powder, and coriander powder.
3. Add salt, tomato and coconut paste and simmer till the oil separates from the mixture.
4. Cook the prawns and whole shallots in the tomato curry and finish with tamarind extract for desired sourness.

Scallops on Tomato Kut

Scallops served on tempered tomato curry

INGREDIENTS

For the tomato kut
8 (1 x 4) Tomatoes, medium-sized
2 tbsp / 30 ml / 1 fl oz Vegetable oil
2 tsp / 10 gm Ginger-garlic (adrak-lasan) paste
1 tsp / 5 gm Red chilli powder
½ tsp / 2½ gm Turmeric (haldi) powder
2 tbsp / 30 gm / 1 oz Gram flour (besan),
   roasted
Salt to taste

For the kut tempering
⅓ cup Vegetable oil
1 tsp / 5 gm Cumin (jeera) seeds
¼ tsp Mustard seeds (rai)
¼ tsp Fenugreek seeds (methi dana)
8 Dry red chillies (sookhi lal mirch)
8 Curry leaves (kadhi patta)

For the scallops
16 King Scallops without shell
2 tbsp / 30 ml / 1 fl oz Lemon (nimbu) juice
Salt to taste
¼ tsp Turmeric powder
1 tbsp / 15 ml Vegetable oil

METHOD

1. **For the tomato kut**, heat the oil in a pan; fry the ginger-garlic paste. Add red chilli powder, turmeric powder, and tomatoes; cook for a few minutes.
2. Mix gram flour in water and add to the cooking tomatoes and simmer for 5 minutes. Blend the tomato mixture and strain. Cook the tomato mixture and add salt.
3. **For the tempering**, heat the oil and add all the tempering ingredients. Pour this mixture into the tomato kut and mix.
4. **For the scallops**, mix lemon juice, salt and turmeric powder with the scallops. Add oil and sear the scallops in a very hot preheated pan. Cook the scallops in the oven or in a salamander and serve on tomato kut.

Soft Shell Crabs

Crispy fried crabs tempered with Tellicherry pepper

INGREDIENTS

For the soft shell crabs
12 Soft shell crabs, cleaned
Salt to taste
2 tbsp / 30 ml / 1 fl oz Lemon (*nimbu*) juice
1 tbsp / 15 gm Ginger-garlic (*adrak-lasan*)
  paste
1 tsp / 5 gm Red chilli powder
2 tbsp / 30 gm / 1 oz Red chilli paste
1 Egg
1 tbsp / 15 gm Cornflour
½ cup / 100 gm / 3½ oz Refined flour (*maida*)
Vegetable oil for frying

For the tempering
4 tsp / 20 ml Vegetable oil
a pinch Asafoetida (*hing*)
4 Dry red chillies (*sookhi lal mirch*), flat
1 tbsp / 15 gm Ginger, julienned
2 Green chillies, slit

15 Curry leaves (*kadhi patta*)
1 tsp / 5 gm Tellicherry pepper, fresh, ground
1 tsp / 5 gm Fennel (*saunf*) powder
1 tsp / 5 ml Lemon juice

METHOD

1. **For the soft shell crabs**, apply salt, lemon juice, and ginger-garlic paste on the crabs and rest them for 5 minutes.
2. Marinate the crabs with red chilli powder, red chilli paste, egg, cornflour, and refined flour.
3. Deep-fry the crabs till crisp.
4. **For the tempering**, heat the oil; add asafoetida, dry red chillies, ginger, green chillies, and curry leaves.
5. Add the crispy fried crabs and sprinkle Tellicherry pepper, fennel powder, and lemon juice.
6. Serve hot.

Tandoori Pink Salmon

Chargrilled salmon served with lemon

INGREDIENTS

8 / 150 gm / 5 oz each Pink salmon, darnes
Salt to taste
2 tbsp / 30 gm / 1 oz Ginger-garlic (adrak-lasan) paste
2 Juice of lemons (nimbu)
1 tsp / 5 gm Red chilli powder
½ cup / 100 gm / 3½ oz Red chilli paste
1 tsp / 5 gm Garam masala powder
1 tbsp / 15 ml Mustard (sarson) oil
1 cup / 200 gm / 7 oz Yoghurt (dahi), hung
1 tsp / 5 gm Bishop's weed (ajwain)
½ cup / 100 gm / 3½ oz Butter for basting
1 tsp / 5 gm Chaat masala

For the accompaniment
2 Onions, cut into rings
4 Lemons, cut into wedges

METHOD

1. Apply salt, ginger-garlic paste, and lemon juice to the fish and rest for 5 minutes.
2. Mix red chilli powder, red chilli paste, salt, garam masala powder, mustard oil, yoghurt and Bishop's weed together.
3. Marinate the fish in the above mixture for 10 minutes.
4. Chargrill the fish basting with butter. Sprinkle chaat masala.
5. Serve with onion rings and lemon wedges.

Tellicherry Fried Prawns

Crispy prawns spiced with Tellicherry pepper

INGREDIENTS

For the fried prawns
32 Prawns (U21-25), shelled with tail
Salt to taste
2 tbsp / 30 ml / 1 fl oz Lemon (*nimbu*) juice
1 tbsp / 15 gm Ginger-garlic (*adrak-lasan*)
   paste
1 tsp / 5 gm Red chilli powder
2 tbsp / 30 gm / 1 oz Red chilli paste
1 Egg
1 tbsp / 15 gm Cornflour
½ cup / 100 gm / 3½ fl oz Refined flour (*maida*)
Vegetable oil for frying

For the tempering
4 tsp / 20 ml Vegetable oil
a pinch Asafoetida (*hing*)
4 Dry red chillies (*sookhi lal mirch*), flat
1 tbsp / 15 gm Ginger, julienned
2 Green chillies, slit
15 Curry leaves (*kadhi patta*)
1 tsp / 5 gm Tellicherry pepper, freshly ground
1 tsp / 5 gm Fennel (*saunf*) seeds, powder
1 tsp / 5 ml Lemon juice

METHOD

1. **For the fried prawns**, apply salt, lemon juice, ginger-garlic paste and rest the prawns for 5 minutes.
2. Marinate the prawns with red chilli powder, red chilli paste, egg, cornflour, and refined flour.
3. Deep-fry the prawns till crisp.
4. **For the tempering**, heat the oil and add asafoetida, dry red chillies, ginger, green chillies, and curry leaves.
5. Add the crispy fried prawns and sprinkle Tellicherry pepper, fennel powder, and lemon juice.
6. Serve hot.

chicken

Chicken Kathi Kebab

Chicken wraps

INGREDIENTS

For the chicken tikka
32 Chicken boneless cubes (*tikka*)
Salt to taste
1 Juice of lemon (*nimbu*)
1 tbsp / 15 gm Garlic-ginger (*lasan-adrak*)
   paste
½ cup / 100 gm / 3½ oz Red chilli paste
1 cup / 200 gm / 7 oz Yoghurt (*dahi*), hung
1 tbsp / 15 ml Mustard (*sarson*) oil
1 tsp / 5 gm *Garam masala* powder

For the salad (*kachumber*)
2 Onions, sliced
2 Tomatoes, deseeded, sliced
2 tbsp / 30 gm / 1 oz Green corainder (*hara
   dhaniya*), chopped
1 tsp / 5 ml Lemon (*nimbu*) juice
Salt to taste

For the wraps
2 cups / 400 gm / 14 oz Refined flour (*maida*)
Salt to taste
1 tsp / 5 gm Sugar
½ cup / 100 ml / 3½ fl oz Milk
1 tsp / 5 gm Baking powder
9 Eggs
½ tsp / 2½ gm Turmeric (*haldi*) powder
1 tbsp / 15 gm Green coriander, chopped
½ cup / 100 ml / 3½ fl oz Vegetable oil
½ tsp / 2½ gm *Chaat masala*
2 tbsp / 30 gm / 1 oz Mint (*pudina*) chutney
8 sheets Butter / Parchment paper (8"x 8")

METHOD

1. **For the chicken tikka**, apply salt, lemon juice, and ginger-garlic paste into the chicken. Rest aside for 20 minutes.
2. Apply red chilli paste, hung yoghurt, mustard oil, *garam masala*, and salt.
3. Cook in a moderately hot Indian clay oven for 8 minutes. Remove, slice and transfer into a bowl.
4. **For the salad (*kachumber*)**, mix onions, tomatoes, green coriander, lemon juice, and salt together.
5. **For the wraps**, make a soft dough with flour, salt, sugar, milk, baking powder, 1 egg, and 1 tbsp oil.
6. Divide the dough into 8 balls of equal size. Roll them into thin sheets and cook on a griddle (*tawa*).
7. Break the remaining eggs in a bowl. Add salt, turmeric powder, and green coriander.
8. Coat the above wraps in the egg batter and fry them on a griddle (*tawa*) using very little oil.
9. Divide the sliced cooked chicken into 8 parts and spread it onto the egg-coated wrap skins followed by salad (*kachumber*), mint chutney, and *chaat masala*.
10. Make chicken rolls and wrap them in parchment papers. Serve hot.

Kali Mirch ka Murga

Pepper chicken in white gravy

INGREDIENTS

For the white gravy
2 tbsp / 30 ml / 1 fl oz Vegetable oil
¼ cup / 50 gm / 2¾ oz Boiled onion paste
1 tbsp / 15 gm Ginger-garlic (adrak-lasan)
  paste
1 cup / 200 gm / 7 oz Cashew nut (kaju) paste
½ cup / 100 gm / 3½ oz Yoghurt (dahi)
Salt to taste

For the chicken
32 Chicken, boneless cubes (tikka)
Salt to taste
1 tbsp / 15 gm Ginger-garlic paste
½ cup / 100 gm / 3½ oz Yoghurt, thick
1 tbsp / 15 ml Vegetable oil
½ tsp / 2½ gm Garam masala powder

For tossing
1 tbsp / 15 ml Vegetable oil
1 small piece Ginger, juliennes
2 Green chillies, slit
2 tbsp / 30 gm / 1 oz Onions, chopped
20 Mint (pudina) leaves, broken
20 Black peppercorns (sabut kali mirch),
  crushed
1 cup / 200 ml / 7 fl oz Stock
½ cup / 100 ml / 3½ fl oz Cream, fresh
½ tsp / 2½ gm Cumin (jeera) powder
½ tsp / 2½ gm Garam masala powder
1 cup / 200 gm / 7 oz Mango (aam) relish

METHOD

1. **For the white gravy**, heat the oil in a pan and fry the onion paste. Add ginger-garlic paste and cook till light brown.
2. Add cashew nut paste, yoghurt and salt. Simmer the gravy till it leaves fat.
3. **For the chicken**, marinate the chicken in salt, ginger-garlic paste, yoghurt, oil, and garam masala. Keep aside for 2 hours.
4. Chargrill the chicken cubes.
5. **For tossing**, heat the oil and fry ginger, green chillies and onions. Toss in the chargrilled chicken followed by the white gravy.
6. Add mint leaves, crushed black peppercorns, and stock.
7. Finish with cream, cumin powder, and garam masala. Serve hot with mango relish

Murg Khatta Pyaz

Chicken morsels in onion-tomato gravy

INGREDIENTS

For the chicken tikka
32 Chicken boneless cubes (*tikka*)
Salt to taste
1 Juice of lemon (*nimbu*)
2 tbsp / 30 gm / 1 oz Ginger-garlic (*adrak-lasan*) paste
½ cup / 100 gm / 3½ gm Red chilli paste
1 tbsp / 15 ml Mustard (*sarson*) oil
1 tsp / 5 gm *Garam masala* powder
1 cup / 200 gm / 7 oz Yoghurt (*dahi*), hung

For the gravy
¼ cup / 50 ml / 1¾ fl oz Vegetable oil
1 tsp / 5 gm Cumin (*jeera*) seeds
1 tbsp / 15 gm Ginger-garlic paste
1 cup / 200 gm / 7 oz Onions, chopped
1 tbsp / 15 gm Red chilli paste
Salt to taste
1 cup / 200 gm / 7 oz Tomatoes, chopped
a pinch Cardamom-mace (*elaichi javitri*) powder
1 tsp / 5 gm Red chilli powder
½ cup / 100 gm / 3½ oz Cashew nut (*kaju*) paste

For tossing
1 tbsp / 15 ml Vegetable oil
1 tsp / 5 gm Cumin seeds
1 tsp / 5 gm Garlic, chopped
1 tsp / 5 gm Ginger, chopped
1 Green chilli, chopped
8 Pickled onions
½ tsp Red chilli flakes
1 tsp / 5 gm *Chaat masala*
a pinch Fenugreek (*methi*) powder
a pinch Cardamom-mace powder
¼ cup / 50 gm / 1¾ oz Green coriander (*hara dhaniya*)

METHOD

1. **For the chicken tikka**, apply salt, lemon juice and ginger-garlic paste and rest the chicken for 20 minutes.
2. Apply red chilli paste, mustard oil, salt, *garam masala*, and hung yoghurt.
3. Cook in a moderately hot Indian clay oven for 8 minutes.
4. **For the gravy**, heat the oil and crackle the cumin seeds. Sauté the ginger-garlic paste, onions, and red chilli paste.
5. Add salt, tomatoes, cardamom-mace powder, red chilli powder, and cashew nut paste. Reserve the gravy.
6. **For tossing**, heat a few drops of oil on a griddle (*tawa*); fry the cumin seeds, garlic, ginger, and green chilli. Add the above gravy, chicken, pickled onions, and red chilli flakes.
7. Finish the chicken with *chaat masala*, fenugreek powder, cardamom-mace powder and green coriander.

Murgi nu Farcha

Crumb fried chicken cubes

INGREDIENTS

24 Chicken boneless cubes (*tikka*)
Salt to taste
½ tsp / 2½ gm Turmeric (*haldi*) powder
1 tsp / 5 gm Red chilli powder
1 tbsp / 15 gm Ginger (*adrak*), chopped
3 cloves Garlic (*lasan*), crushed
¼ tsp *Garam masala* powder
1 cup / 200 gm / 7 oz Tomato paste
1 Juice of lemon
2 tbsp / 30 gm / 1 oz Tomato ketchup
1 tbsp / 15 ml Vegetable oil
2 cups / 400 gm / 14 oz Breadcrumbs
6 Eggs, beaten
Vegetable oil for frying

METHOD

1. Marinate chicken in salt, turmeric powder, red chilli powder, ginger, garlic, *garam masala* powder, tomato paste, lemon juice, tomato ketchup, and oil for at least 3 hours.
2. Cook the marinated chicken in a pan. Cool down the chicken. Remove chicken pieces and strain the pan extract.
3. Reserve the pan juices to serve as sauce with the *farcha*.
4. Crumb the chicken, coat with beaten eggs and deep-fry till golden.
5. Serve the *farcha* with the above sauce.

Tikka Pita

Boneless chicken in pita bread topped with salad

INGREDIENTS

For the chicken tikka
32 Chicken boneless cubes (*tikka*)
1 Juice of lemon (*nimbu*)
1 tbsp / 15 gm Ginger-garlic (*adrak-lasan*)
   paste
½ cup / 100 gm / 3½ oz Red chilli paste
1 cup / 200 gm / 7 oz Yoghurt (*dahi*), hung
1 tbsp / 15 ml Mustard (*sarson*) oil
1 tsp / 5 gm *Garam masala* powder
Salt to taste

For the salad (*kachumber*)
2 Onions, sliced
2 Tomatoes, deseeded, sliced
2 tbsp / 30 gm / 1 oz Green coriander (*hara
   dhaniya*), chopped
1 tsp / 5 ml Lemon (*nimbu*) juice
Salt to taste

For the presentation
4 Pita bread (6")

METHOD

1. **For the chicken tikka**, apply salt, lemon juice, and ginger-garlic paste on the chicken cubes. Rest aside for 20 mintues.
2. Apply red chilli paste, yoghurt, mustard oil, salt, and *garam masala*.
3. Cook in a moderately hot Indian clay oven for 8 minutes. Remove, slice and transfer in a bowl.
4. **For the salad** (*kachumber*), mix all the ingredients mentioned.
5. **For the presentation**, cut the pita bread into two. Open the pita pockets and fill ¾th with chicken tikka and top with salad.

Malai Tikka on Khasta Roti

Chicken morsels on crispy bread coins

INGREDIENTS

For the first marinade
1.5 kg / 3.3 lb Chicken boneless, cut into 2.5"
  cubes
1 tbsp / 15 ml Lemon (*nimbu*) juice
2 tbsp / 36 gm / 1¼ oz Ginger-garlic (*adrak-lasan*) paste
1 tsp / 5 gm Salt

For the final marinade
1 cup / 250 gm / 9 oz Cheddar cheese, grated
  (Amul)
2 Egg yolks
1 cup / 200 ml / 7 fl oz Cream (45% fat), fresh
½ cup / 100 gm / 3½ oz Yoghurt (*dahi*), hung
½ cup / 100 gm / 3½ oz Cashew nut (*kaju*) paste
¼ cup / 50 gm / 1¾ oz Mint (*pudina*) leaves,
  finely chopped
2 Green chillies, chopped
2 tbsp / 30 ml / 1 fl oz Vegetable oil
½ tsp / 2½ gm White pepper (*safed mirch*)
  powder
½ tsp / 2½ gm Cardamom-mace (*elaichi-javitri*)
  powder
½ cup / 100 gm / 3½ oz Butter yellow (for
  basting)

For the bread coins (*khasta roti*): makes 24
1 cup / 200 gm / 7 oz Semolina (*suji*)
3 cups / 600 gm / 22 oz Wholewheat flour (*atta*)
1 tbsp / 15 gm Shortening
a pinch Salt
Water to bind

For the presentation
1 tsp / 5 gm *Chaat masala*
4 Juice of lemons (*nimbu*)
½ cup / 100 gm / 3½ oz Onion rings
½ cup / 100 gm / 3½ oz Carrot (*gajar*) curls
½ cup / 100 gm / 3½ oz Beetroot (*chukandar*)
  curls

METHOD

1. Wash and pat dry the chicken. In a bowl mix lemon juice, ginger-garlic paste, and salt and rest the chicken cubes for 20 minutes.

2. In a bowl add grated cheddar cheese, egg yolks, cream, yoghurt, cashew nut paste, mint leaves, green chillies, oil, white pepper and cardamom-mace powder. Rest for 10 minutes for the cheese to soften. Lightly whisk the mixture to get a smooth texture.

3. Drain out the excess liquid from the chicken and add the chicken to the cream and cheese mix. Keep refrigerated for a minimum of 6 hours.

4. Cook the chicken cubes in a tandoor basting regularly with butter.

5. **For the bread coins**, mix all the ingredients mentioned and knead into a dough. Roll and cut with a cutter into 1½" diameter. Bake till golden brown.

6. Serve the grilled chicken hot sprinkled with *chaat masala* and lemon juice and accompanied with mint chutney, onion rings, and vegetable curls on crispy bread coins.

lamb

Bombay Gotala

Lamb mince, kidney and liver delicacy

INGREDIENTS

2 cups / 400 gm / 14 oz Lamb mince
½ cup / 100 gm / 3½ oz Lamb kidney
½ cup / 100 gm / 3½ oz Lamb liver, soaked in
  milk
¼ cup / 50 ml / 1¾ fl oz Vegetable oil
½ cup / 100 gm / 3½ oz Onions, chopped
1 tbsp / 15 gm Ginger-garlic (*adrak-lasan*)
  paste
1 tsp / 5 gm Green chillies, chopped
1 tsp / 5 gm Red chilli powder
1 tbsp / 15 gm Coriander (*dhaniya*) powder
¼ cup / 50 gm / 1¾ oz Tomatoes, chopped
Salt to taste
½ tsp / 2½ gm *Garam masala* powder
1 tsp / 5 ml Lemon (*nimbu*) juice
¼ cup / 50 gm / 1¾ oz Green coriander (*hara
  dhaniya*), chopped

METHOD

1. Heat the oil in a pan; fry the onions,
   ginger-garlic paste, green chillies, red chilli
   powder, coriander powder, and tomatoes.
2. Add mince and cook. Add kidney, liver,
   and salt; simmer for 15 minutes.
3. Sprinkle *garam masala* and finish with
   lemon juice and green coriander.

Dum ki Chaampen

Seared lamb chops

INGREDIENTS

24 Kid lamb chops
1 cup / 200 ml / 7 fl oz Vegetable oil
6 Onions, sliced
1 tbsp / 15 gm Ginger-garlic (*adrak-lasan*) paste
2 Green chillies
2 tsp / 10 gm Coriander (*dhaniya*) powder
1 tsp / 5 gm Red chilli powder
3 Tomatoes, sliced
½ cup / 100 gm / 3½ oz Cashew nut (*kaju*) paste
1 tsp / 5 gm Cumin (*jeera*) seeds
6 Green cardamoms (*choti elaichi*)
2 Bay leaves (*tej patta*)
8 Cloves (*laung*)
Salt to taste
a few strands Saffron (*kesar*)
½ tsp / 2½ gm *Garam masala* powder

METHOD

1. Heat ½ cup oil in a pan; fry the onions till light golden. Add ginger-garlic paste, green chillies, coriander powder, and red chilli powder; fry. Add tomatoes and cook.
2. Add cashew nut paste and 2 cups water; mix well. Simmer for 20 minutes.
3. Blend to a fine paste and strain.
4. Heat the remaining oil in a heavy-bottomed pan; fry the cumin seeds, green cardamoms, bay leaves, and cloves. Sear the lamb chops and add the blended curry to the shanks. Simmer the shanks till cooked.
5. Season the lamb chops and finish with roasted saffron strands and *garam masala* powder.
6. Serve hot garnished with green coriander sprigs.

Dum ki Nalli

Lamb shanks served with spicy baked potatoes

INGREDIENTS

For the lamb shanks
8 Kid lambs shanks
1 cup / 200 ml / 7 fl oz Vegetable oil
6 Onions, sliced
1 tbsp / 15 gm Ginger-garlic (*adrak-lasan*) paste
2 Green chillies
2 tsp / 10 gm Coriander (*dhaniya*) powder
1 tsp / 5 gm Red chilli powder
3 Tomatoes, sliced
½ cup / 100 gm / 3½ oz Cashew nut (*kaju*) paste
1 tsp / 5 gm Cumin (*jeera*) seeds
6 Green cardamoms (*choti elaichi*)
2 Bay leaves (*tej patta*)
8 Cloves (*laung*)
½ tsp / 2½ gm *Garam masala* powder
a few strands Saffron (*kesar*)

For the spicy baked potatoes
500 gm / 1.1 lb Potatoes, sliced, parboiled
1 tbsp / 15 gm Butter
1 cup / 200 gm / 7 oz Chedder cheese
4 Eggs
Salt to taste
½ tsp / 2½ gm Turmeric (*haldi*) powder
½ tsp / 2½ gm Cumin powder
2 cups / 400 ml / 14 fl oz Cream

For the presentation
8 sprigs Green coriander (*hara dhaniya*)
4 Gold leaves (*varq*)

METHOD

1. Heat ½ cup oil in a pan; fry the onions till light golden. Fry ginger-garlic paste, green chillies, coriander powder, and red chilli powder. Add tomatoes and cook.
2. Add cashew nut paste and 2 cups of water to the pan. Simmer for 20 minutes.
3. Blend to a fine paste and strain.
4. Heat the remaining oil in a heavy-bottomed pan; fry cumin seeds, green cardamoms, bay leaves, and cloves. Sear the lamb shanks and add the blended curry to the shanks. Simmer the shanks till cooked.
5. Season the lamb shanks and finish with roasted saffron strands and *garam masala* powder.
6. **For the spicy baked potatoes**, grease a baking tin with butter and layer with potatoes and cheese. Beat the eggs and mix in salt, turmeric powder, cumin powder, and cream. Pour this mixture over the potatoes and bake at 180°C / 350°F for 25 minutes.
7. Serve hot lamb shanks with baked potatoes garnished with green corainder and gold leaves.

Keema Toasty

Minced lamb toasts

INGREDIENTS

2 cups / 400 gm / 14 oz Lamb mince
¼ cup / 50 gm / 1¾ fl oz Vegetable oil
½ cup / 100 gm / 3½ oz Onions, chopped
1 tbsp / 15 gm Ginger-garlic (*adrak-lasan*)
  paste
1 tsp / 5 gm Green chillies, chopped
1 tsp / 5 gm Red chilli powder
1 tbsp / 15 gm Coriander (*dhaniya*) powder
¼ cup / 50 gm / 1¾ oz Tomatoes, chopped
Salt to taste
½ tsp / 2½ gm *Garam masala* powder
1 tsp / 5 ml Lemon (*nimbu*) juice
¼ cup / 50 gm / 1¾ oz Green coriander (*hara
  dhaniya*), chopped
8 White bread, slices
1 tbsp / 15 gm Butter

METHOD

1. Heat the oil in a pan; fry the onions,
   ginger-garlic paste, green chillies, red chilli
   powder, coriander powder, and tomatoes.
2. Add mince and cook. Add salt and simmer
   for 15 minutes.
3. Sprinkle *garam masala* and finish with
   lemon juice and green coriander. Cool the
   mixture.
4. Make toasty sandwiches with lamb mince.

vegetarian

Achari Broccoli

Pickled broccoli

INGREDIENTS

600 gm / 22 oz Broccoli, cleaned, blanched
½ cup / 100 gm / 3½ oz Yoghurt (*dahi*), thick
2 tbsp / 30 gm / 1 oz Pickle paste
¼ tsp Turmeric (*haldi*) powder
1 tbsp / 15 ml Vegetable oil
½ tsp / 2½ gm Onion seeds (*kalonji*)
1 tsp / 5 gm *Chaat masala*
1 Juice of lemon (*nimbu*)

For the presentation
½ cup / 100 gm / 3½ oz Onion rings
½ cup / 100 gm / 3½ oz Carrot (*gajar*) curls
½ cup / 100 gm / 3½ oz Beetroot (*chukandar*)
  curls

METHOD

1. Marinate the broccoli florets in yoghurt, pickle paste, turmeric powder, and oil. Rest for 20 minutes.
2. Cook the broccoli in a tandoor and serve hot sprinkled with onion seeds, *chaat masala*, and lemon juice; and garnished with onion, carrot and beetroot curls.

Aloo Anardana

Potatoes with pomegranate seeds

INGREDIENTS

4 cups Potatoes, cut into 2.5" cubes
¼ cup / 50 ml / 1¾ fl oz Vegetable oil
¼ tsp Cumin (*jeera*) seeds
1 tbsp / 15 gm Ginger-garlic (*adrak-lasan*) paste
1 tsp / 5 gm Green chillies, chopped
½ tsp / 2½ gm Turmeric (*haldi*) powder
Salt to taste
1 tsp / 5 gm Dry pomegranate seed (*anar dana*) powder
½ tsp / 2½ gm *Chaat masala*
½ cup / 100 gm / 3½ oz Pomegranate seeds, fresh
1 tbsp / 15 gm Green coriander (*hara dhaniya*), chopped
½ tsp / 2½ gm Lemon (*nimbu*) juice

METHOD

1. Heat the oil in a pan; fry the cumin seeds, ginger-garlic paste, green chillies, turmeric powder, salt, pomegranate seed powder, and potatoes. Cook the potatoes, covered, on moderate heat or in an oven at 200°C / 400°F C for 20 minutes.

2. Sprinkle *chaat masala* and add fresh pomegranate seeds, green coriander and lemon juice. Serve hot.

Aloo Karwari

Deep-fried potatoes served with coconut chutney

INGREDIENTS

For the potatoes
32 Baby potatoes, boiled in turmeric water
Salt to taste
2 tbsp / 30 ml / 1 fl oz Lemon (*nimbu*) juice
1 tbsp / 15 gm Ginger-garlic (*adrak-lasan*) paste
1 tsp / 5 gm Red chilli powder
1 tbsp / 15 gm Red chilli paste
1 tsp / 5 gm Cumin (*jeera*) powder
1 tsp / 5 gm Turmeric (*haldi*) powder
1 Egg
½ cup / 100 gm / 3½ oz Tamarind (*imli*), soaked
2 cups / 400 gm / 14 oz Semolina (*sooji*), white

For the chutney
1 cup / 200 gm / 7 oz Coconut (*nariyal*), fresh,
  grated
4 Kashmiri chillies, dried
4 Dry red chillies (*sookhi lal mirch*), button
6 Curry leaves (*kadhi patta*)

a pinch Asafoetida (*hing*)
1 tbsp / 15 ml Vegetable oil for tempering
Vegetable oil for frying

METHOD

1. **For the potatoes**, to the soft boiled
    potatoes apply salt, lemon juice, and
    ginger-garlic paste. Rest for 15 minutes.
2. Add red chilli powder, red chilli paste,
    cumin powder, turmeric powder, egg, and
    tamarind extract.
3. Coat the potatoes with semolina and press
    between palms. Deep-fry in moderately
    hot oil and serve hot with coconut chutney.
4. **For the chutney**, make a fine paste of
    grated coconut and Kashmiri chillies and
    temper with button chillies, asafoetida and
    curry leaves.

Aloo Katliyan

Potato roundels

INGREDIENTS

1 kg / 2.2 lb Potatoes, sliced
Salt to taste
1 tsp / 5 gm Turmeric (haldi) powder
1 tbsp / 15 ml Vegetable oil
1 tsp / 5 gm Cumin (jeera) seeds
½ tsp / 2½ gm Bishop's weed (ajwain)
½ tsp / 2½ gm Asafoetida (hing)
8 Curry leaves (kadhi patta), shredded
1 tsp / 5 gm Red chilli flakes
1 tsp / 5 gm Garlic (lasan), chopped
1 tsp / 5 gm Ginger (adrak), chopped
1 Green chilli, chopped
1 tsp / 5 gm Chaat masala
2 tbsp / 30 gm / 1 oz Green coriander (hara dhaniya), chopped
1 Juice of lemon (nimbu)

METHOD

1. Boil the potatoes with salt and turmeric powder.
2. Heat the oil on a hot plate; add cumin seeds, Bishop's weed, asafoetida, curry leaves, red chilli flakes, garlic, ginger, and green chilli.
3. Add boiled potatoes and sprinkle chaat masala, green coriander, and lemon juice.
4. Stir-fry and serve hot.

Baingan Saraf

Mashed and spiced aubergine

INGREDIENTS

4 cups Aubergine (*baingan*), roasted, mashed
2 tbsp / 30 ml / 1 fl oz Vegetable oil
1 cup / 200 gm / 7 oz Onions, cut into cubes
1 cup / 200 gm / 7 oz Tomatoes, cut into cubes
1 tbsp / 15 gm Ginger (*adrak*), chopped
2 Green chillies, slit
1 tsp / 5 gm Red chilli powder
Salt to taste
1 tbsp / 15 gm Butter
1 tbsp / 15 gm Green coriander (*hara dhaniya*),
  chopped

For the presentation
4 Aubergine shells, roasted / fried

METHOD

1. Heat the oil in a pan; fry the onions, tomatoes, ginger, green chillies, and red chilli powder.
2. Add mashed aubergine, salt, and butter and cook for 8-10 minutes.
3. Add green coriander and serve the mash in roasted or fried aubergine shells.

Bhindi Naintara

Okra flavoured with coconut

INGREDIENTS

4 cups Okra (bhindi), cut into 2 cm pieces
2 tbsp / 30 ml / 1 fl oz Vegetable oil
1 tbsp / 15 gm Ginger (adrak), chopped
½ tsp / 2½ gm Green chillies, chopped
1 cup / 200 gm / 7 oz Onions, diced
½ tsp / 2½ gm Turmeric (haldi) powder
Salt to taste
½ cup / 100 gm / 3½ oz Tomatoes, diced
1 tbsp / 15 gm Black and white sesame (til) seeds
1 tbsp / 15 gm Coconut (nariyal), grated

For the presentation
10 Coconut, fresh, cut into slices
1 tsp / 5 gm Black and white sesame seeds

METHOD

1. Heat the oil in a wok (kadhai); fry ginger, green chillies, and onions. Add turmeric powder, salt and okra and cook on low heat.
2. Add tomatoes, sesame seeds, and coconut; and cook, covered, on low heat.
3. Serve garnished with sesame seeds and coconut slices.

Candied Batata Wada

Potato fritters stuffed with sugarcane candies

INGREDIENTS

400 gm / 14 oz Potatoes, boiled, mashed
1 tsp / 5 gm Mustard seeds (*rai*)
½ tsp / 2½ gm Asafoetida (*hing*) powder
8 Curry leaves (*kadhi patta*)
2 pods Garlic (*lasan*), crushed
½ tsp / 2½ gm Turmeric (*haldi*) powder
1 tbsp / 15 gm Ginger (*adrak*), chopped
1 tsp / 5 gm Green chillies, chopped
Salt to taste
3 Eggs, beaten
2 cups / 400 gm / 14 oz Fresh bread croutons
16 Sugarcane candies, 3" long
2 tbsp / 30 ml / 1 fl oz Vegetable oil for frying

For the accompaniment
½ cup / 100 gm / 3½ oz Tamarind (*imli*) relish

METHOD

1. Temper the mashed potatoes with mustard seeds, asafoetida, curry leaves, garlic, turmeric powder, ginger, and green chillies. Add salt.
2. Divide the potato mix into 16 portions; coat each with egg and fresh bread croutons. Insert sugarcane candies into each potato fritter.
3. Deep-fry the potato fritters. Serve hot in shot glasses with tamarind relish.

Chilgoza Falli

Haricot beans cooked with pine nuts and cherry tomatoes

INGREDIENTS

800 gm / 28 oz Haricot verte, cut into 2″-long
   pieces
1 tbsp / 15 ml Olive oil
1 tsp / 5 gm Cumin (*jeera*) seeds
1 tsp / 5 gm Garlic (*lasan*), chopped
1 tsp / 5 gm Ginger (*adrak*), chopped
1 Green chilli, chopped
½ tsp / 2½ gm Red chilli flakes
1 tbsp / 15 gm Pine nuts (*chilgoza*), shelled
8 Cherry tomatoes, halved
1 tsp / 5 gm *Chaat masala*
1 Juice of lemon (*nimbu*)
Salt to taste

METHOD

1. Blanch the haricot in salt water and reserve
    in chilled water.
2. Heat the oil and crackle the cumin seeds.
    Stir in garlic, ginger, and green chilli.
3. Add red chilli flakes, pine nuts, and haricot;
    and stir-fry.
4. Add cherry tomatoes and finish with *chaat
    masala* and lemon juice.

Chonke Khatte Mutter

Tempered green peas

INGREDIENTS

4 cups Green peas (*hara mutter*), fresh, boiled
2 tbsp / 30 ml / 1 fl oz Vegetable oil
½ tsp / 2½ gm Cumin (*jeera*) seeds
¼ cup / 50 gm / 1¾ oz Onion, chopped
1 tsp / 5 gm Ginger (*adrak*), chopped
½ tsp / 2½ gm Green chillies, chopped
¼ tsp Turmeric (*haldi*), powder
8 (1 x 2) Baby tomatoes
Salt to taste
1 tsp / 5 gm Dry mango powder (*amchur*)
½ tsp / 2½ gm *Chaat masala*
1 tsp / 5 ml Lemon (*nimbu*) juice
1 tbsp / 15 gm Green coriander (*hara dhaniya*),
   chopped

METHOD

1. Heat the oil on a griddle (*tawa*); fry cumin
   seeds, onion, ginger, green chillies, and
   turmeric powder.
2. Add boiled green peas, tomatoes, salt, dry
   mango powder, and *chaat masala*.
3. Finish with lemon juice and green
   coriander.

Gobhi Broccoli

Stir-fried cauliflower and broccoli

INGREDIENTS

3 cups Cauliflower (*phool gobhi*), cut into florets
2 cups Broccoli, cut into florets
2 tbsp / 30 ml / 1 fl oz Vegetable oil
½ tsp / 2½ oz Cumin (*jeera*) seeds
2 tbsp / 30 gm / 1 oz Ginger (*adrak*), juliennes
1 tbsp / 15 gm Ginger-garlic (*adrak-lasan*) paste
2 Green chillies, slit
1 tsp / 5 gm Turmeric (*haldi*) powder
Salt to taste
8 Red cherry tomatoes
1 tsp / 5 gm *Chaat masala*
1 tbsp / 15 gm Green coriander (*hara dhaniya*), chopped
1 tbsp / 15 ml Lemon (*nimbu*) juice

METHOD

1. Heat the oil in a pan; fry the cumin seeds, ginger, ginger-garlic paste, and green chillies.
2. Add turmeric powder, cauliflower, and salt. Cook, covered, for 10 minutes.
3. Add broccoli and cherry tomatoes; stir on high heat for 5 minutes. Check cauliflower for doneness and finish with *chaat masala*, green coriander and lemon juice.

Gucchi Khumb

Mushrooms in tomato gravy

INGREDIENTS

For the gravy
¼ cup / 50 ml / 1¾ fl oz Vegetable oil
1 tsp / 5 gm Cumin (*jeera*) seeds
1 cup / 200 gm / 7 oz Onions, chopped
1 tbsp / 15 gm Ginger-garlic (*adrak-lasan*) paste
1 tsp / 5 gm Red chilli powder
1 cup / 200 gm / 7 oz Tomatoes, chopped
½ cup / 100 gm / 3½ oz Cashew nut (*kaju*)
   paste
Salt to taste

For stir-frying
400 gm / 14 oz Mushrooms (*gucchi*)
12 Morels, washed, soaked, cut into small
   pieces
1 tbsp / 15 ml Vegetable oil
1 tsp / 5 gm Garlic, chopped
1 tsp / 5 gm Ginger, chopped
1 Green chilli, chopped
1 tbsp / 15 gm Spring onions (*hara pyaz*),
   chopped
1 tsp / 5 gm *Chaat masala*
1 tbsp / 15 gm Green coriander (*hara dhaniya*),
   chopped
Salt to taste
a pinch Dry fenugreek powder (*kasoori methi*)

METHOD

1. **For the gravy**, heat the oil and crackle the cumin seeds.
2. Add onions, ginger-garlic paste, red chilli powder followed by tomatoes.
3. Cook for a while and add cashew nut paste and salt.
4. **For stir-frying**, blanch the mushrooms.
5. Heat the oil on a griddle (*tawa*); fry garlic, ginger, and green chilli.
6. Stir in mushrooms and morels. Add the gravy, spring onions, *chaat masala*, and green coriander.
7. Season and finish with dry fenugreek powder.

Khumb Kofta Curry

Mushroom koftas in yoghurt sauce

INGREDIENTS

For the koftas
2 cups / 400 gm / 14 oz Mushrooms, button, shredded
½ cup / 100 gm / 3½ oz Potatoes, boiled, mashed
1 tsp / 5 gm Ginger (adrak), chopped
½ tsp / 2½ gm Green chillies, chopped
Salt to taste
Vegetable oil for frying

For the kofta curry
2 tbsp / 30 ml / 1 fl oz Vegetable oil
2 tbsp / 30 gm / 1 oz Onion, chopped
1 tsp / 5 gm Ginger-garlic (adrak-lasan) paste
2 Green chillies, slit
1 cup / 200 gm / 7 oz Cashew nut (kaju) paste
2 tbsp / 30 gm / 1 oz Poppy seed (khus khus) paste
¼ cup / 50 gm / 1¾ oz Yoghurt (dahi), beaten
1 (1 x 4) Tomato
1 tbsp / 15 gm Onion, browned
1 cup / 200 gm / 7 oz Boiled mushroom paste
¼ tsp Garam masala powder
a few strands Saffron (kesar), soaked in warm water

1 tbsp / 15 gm Green coriander (hara dhaniya), chopped
2 tbsp / 30 gm / 1 oz Cream, fresh
1 tbsp / 15 gm Butter

METHOD

1. **For the koftas**, mix all the ingredients mentioned (except oil) and knead into a smooth mixture. Divide the mixture equally into 16 portions and shape each into a sphere. Deep-fry the spheres till golden. Keep aside to cool.

2. **For the kofta curry**, heat the oil in a pan; fry the onion, ginger-garlic paste, and green chillies. Add cashew nut and poppy seed pastes followed by yoghurt, tomato, and brown onion. Add mushroom paste and simmer the curry for 30 minutes.

3. Add garam masala powder and strain the curry. Finish the curry by adding saffron mixture, green coriander, cream, mushroom koftas, and butter.

Khumb Varqui

Mushrooms in tomato gravy layered with phyllo sheets

INGREDIENTS

For the gravy
¼ cup / 50 ml / 1¾ fl oz Vegetable oil
1 tsp / 5 gm Cumin (*jeera*) seeds
1 cup / 200 gm / 7 oz Onions, chopped
1 tbsp / 15 gm Ginger-garlic (*adrak-lasan*) paste
1 tsp / 5 gm Red chilli powder
1 cup / 200 gm / 7 oz Tomatoes, chopped
½ cup / 100 gm / 3½ oz Cashew nut (*kaju*)
　paste
Salt to taste

For stir-frying
400 gm / 14 oz Mushrooms
12 Morels, washed, soaked, cut into small
　pieces
1 tbsp / 15 ml Vegetable oil
1 tsp / 5 gm Garlic, chopped
1 tsp / 5 gm Ginger, chopped
1 Green chilli, chopped
1 tbsp / 15 gm Spring onions (*hara pyaz*),
　chopped
1 tsp / 5 gm *Chaat masala*
1 tbsp / 15 gm Green coriander (*hara dhaniya*),
　chopped
1 gm Saffron (*kesar*), soaked in warm water
a pinch Fenugreek (*kasoori methi*) powder
Salt to taste

For the presentation
4 Morels (stuffed with cottage cheese)
12 Fresh red chilli rings
4 Fresh red chilli flowers
4 sprigs Green coriander (*hara dhaniya*)
8 Chives
¼ cup / 50 ml / 1¾ fl oz Chilli oil
15 Baked phyllo sheets (7 cm sq)

METHOD

1. **For the gravy**, heat the oil and crackle the cumin seeds.
2. Add onions, ginger-garlic paste, red chilli powder followed by tomatoes.
3. Cook for a while and add cashew nut paste and salt.
4. **For stir-frying**, blanch the mushrooms.
5. Heat the oil on a griddle (*tawa*); fry garlic, ginger and green chilli.
6. Stir in mushrooms and morels. Add gravy, spring onions, *chaat masala*, green coriander, and saffron.
7. Season and finish with fenugreek powder.
8. Present the mushroom mille feuille as shown in the photograph. (Interlayer the filo sheets with the mushroom mixture and garnish with red chilli flower.)

Lal Mirch ka Paneer

Skewered cottage cheese garnished with red chiilies

INGREDIENTS

16 / 800 gm / 28 oz Cottage cheese (*malai paneer*) wheels, cut into 2.5" diameter
½ cup / 100 gm / 3½ oz Mint (*pudina*) chutney
½ cup / 100 gm / 3½ oz Tomato and garlic chutney
Salt to taste
½ tsp / 2½ gm Turmeric (*haldi*) powder
1 cup / 200 gm / 7 oz Yoghurt (*dahi*), thick
½ tsp / 2½ gm Fennel (*saunf*) powder
½ tsp / 2½ gm Yellow chilli powder
½ cup / 100 gm / 3½ oz Cashew nut (*kaju*) paste
¼ tsp *Garam masala* powder
1 tbsp / 15 ml Vegetable oil
1 tbsp / 15 gm *Chaat masala*
1 Juice of lemon (*nimbu*)

For the presentation
1 tsp / 5 gm *Chaat masala*
4 Fried red chillies

METHOD

1. Slit cottage cheese wheels into two layers and line with mint chutney and tomato-garlic chutney separately.
2. Marinate the cottage cheese with salt, turmeric powder, yoghurt, fennel powder, yellow chilli powder, cashew nut paste, *garam masala* powder, and oil.
3. Skewer the cottage cheese and cook in the tandoor for 5 minutes.
4. Sprinkle *chaat masala* and lemon juice. Serve hot garnished with fried red chillies.

PKB Chaat

Tangy dry fruit mix served with tamarind chutney

INGREDIENTS

½ cup / 100 gm / 3½ oz Pistachios (*pista*),
  roasted
½ cup / 100 gm / 3½ oz Cashew nut (*kaju*),
  whole, roasted
½ cup / 100 gm / 3½ oz Almonds (*badam*),
  roasted
½ tsp / 2½ gm *Kala chaat masala*
¼ tsp Red chilli powder
½ tsp / 2½ gm Cumin (*jeera*) powder
1 tbsp / 15 ml Lemon (*nimbu*) juice
2 tbsp / 30 gm / 1 oz Tamarind (*imli*) chutney
2 tbsp / 30 gm / 1 oz Onions, chopped
2 tbsp / 30 gm / 1 oz Tomatoes, chopped
1 tbsp / 15 gm Green coriander (*hara dhaniya*),
  chopped

For the presentation
1 cup / 200 gm / 7 oz Yoghurt (*dahi*) raita
¼ cup / 50 gm / 1¾ oz Tamarind (*imli*) chutney

METHOD

1. Toss pistachios, cashew nuts, and almonds
    in a bowl with the remaining ingredients
2. Present the PKB chaat with *raita* dotted
    with tamarind chutney as shown in the
    photograph.

Dilli ki Challi

Spiced corn on cob

INGREDIENTS

4 Corn on cobs, yellow, boiled
1 tbsp / 15 ml Vegetable oil
1 tsp / 5 gm Ginger (*adrak*)
¼ tsp Red chilli flakes
½ tsp / 2½ gm *Chaat masala*
½ tsp / 2½ gm *Meat masala*
1 tsp / 5 gm Green coriander (*hara dhaniya*),
   chopped
1 tsp / 5 ml Lemon (*nimbu*) juice

For the presentation
½ cup / 100 gm / 3½ oz Onion rings
½ cup / 100 gm / 3½ oz Carrot (*gajar*) curls
½ cup / 100 gm / 3½ oz Beetroot (*chukundar*)
   curls

METHOD

1. Heat the oil in a wok (*kadhai*); fry ginger,
    chilli flakes, corn on the cob, and *chaat
    masala*. Add *meat masala*, green coriander
    and lemon juice
2   Serve hot with onion, carrot, and beetroot
    curls.

Paneer Khatta Pyaz

Cottage cheese and pickled onions in tomato gravy

INGREDIENTS

400 gm / 14 oz Cottage cheese (*paneer*)

For the gravy
¼ cup / 50 ml / 1¾ fl oz Vegetable oil
1 tsp / 5 gm Cumin (*jeera*) seeds
1 tbsp / 15 gm Ginger-garlic (*adrak-lasan*) paste
1 cup / 200 gm / 7 oz Onions, chopped
1 tbsp / 15 gm Red chilli paste
1 cup / 200 gm / 7 oz Tomatoes, chopped
Salt to taste
a pinch Cardamom-mace (*elaichi-javitri*)
   powder
1 tsp / 5 gm Red chilli powder
½ cup / 100 gm / 3½ oz Cashew nut (*kaju*)
   paste

For tossing
1 tbsp / 15 ml Vegetable oil
1 tsp / 5 gm Cumin seeds
1 tsp / 5 gm Garlic, chopped
1 tsp / 5 gm Ginger, chopped
1 Green chilli, chopped
8 Pickled onions
½ tsp / 2½ gm Red chilli flakes
1 tsp / 5 gm *Chaat masala*
a pinch Fenugreek (*methi*) powder
¼ cup / 50 gm / 1¾ oz Green coriander (*hara
   dhaniya*)

METHOD

1. **For the gravy**, heat the oil; crackle cumin
    seeds and sauté ginger-garlic paste,
    onions, and red chilli paste. Add salt,
    tomatoes, cardamom-mace powder,
    red chilli powder, and cashew nut paste.
    Reserve the gravy.
2. **For tossing**, heat a few drops of oil on
    a griddle *(tawa)*; fry cumin seeds, garlic,
    ginger, and green chilli. Add the tomato
    gravy, cottage cheese, pickled onions, and
    red chilli flakes.
3. Finish the cottage cheese with *chaat
    masala*, fenugreek powder, and green
    coriander.

Mutter Tikki Chaat

Green pea patties served with yoghurt, tamarind and mint relish

INGREDIENTS

2 cups / 400 gm / 14 oz Green peas (*hara mutter*), shelled, boiled, mashed
½ cup / 100 gm / 3½ oz Potatoes, boiled, mashed
2 tbsp / 30 ml / 1 fl oz Vegetable oil for tempering
½ tsp / 2½ gm Cumin (*jeera*) seeds
1 tbsp / 15 gm Ginger (*adrak*), chopped
1 tsp / 5 gm Green chilli, chopped
Salt to taste
1 tsp / 5 gm Raw mango powder (*amchoor*)
1 tbsp / 15 gm Green coriander (*hara dhaniya*), chopped
Vegetable oil for shallow-frying

For the presentation
1 tsp / 5 gm Red chilli powder
1 tsp / 5 gm Cumin powder
1 tsp / 5 gm *Kala chaat masala*
½ cup / 100 gm / 3½ oz Yoghurt (*dahi*), beaten
½ cup / 100 gm / 3½ oz Tamarind (*imli*) chutney
¼ cup / 50 gm / 1¾ oz Mint (*pudina*) chutney

METHOD

1. Mix the mashed green peas and potatoes together. Temper with oil, cumin seeds, ginger, and green chilli.
2. Season the mixture with salt and raw mango powder. Add green coriander.
3. Make patties with the mixture and shallow-fry till crisp.
4. Present the green pea patties with red chilli powder, cumin powder, *kala chaat masala*, yoghurt, tamarind chutney, and mint chutney.

Paneer Parcha

Cottage cheese rolls in white fenugreek curry

INGREDIENTS

For the cottage cheese rolls
16 Cottage cheese (*paneer*), cut into 7 cm x
   7 cm sheets
1 cup / 200 gm / 7 oz Cottage cheese, mashed
1 tbsp / 15 ml Vegetable oil
½ tsp / 2½ gm Cumin (*jeera*) seeds
2 tbsp / 30 gm / 1 oz Onions, chopped
1 tbsp / 15 gm Tomatoes, chopped
1 tsp / 5 gm Ginger (*adrak*), chopped
1 tsp / 5 gm Green chillies, chopped
½ tsp / 2½ gm Turmeric (*haldi*) powder
1 tbsp / 15 gm Green coriander (*hara dhaniya*),
   chopped
Salt to taste

For the white fenugreek curry
2 tbsp / 30 ml / 1 fl oz Vegetable oil
2 Green cardamoms (*choti elaichi*)
1 Cinnamon (*dalchini*) stick
1 tbsp / 15 gm Onion, chopped
1 tsp / 5 gm Ginger, chopped
½ tsp / 2½ gm Green chillies, chopped
1 cup / 200 gm / 7 oz Cashew nut (*kaju*) paste
2 tbsp / 30 gm / 1 oz Yoghurt (*dahi*), beaten
Salt to taste
2 tbsp / 30 gm / 1 oz Cream
¼ cup / 50 gm / 1¾ oz Dry fenugreek leaves
   (*kasoori methi*)
4 Scallion greens, blanched

METHOD

1. **For the white fenugreek curry**, heat the
    oil in a pan; fry the green cardamoms,
    cinnamon stick, onion, ginger, and green
    chillies. Add cashew nut paste, beaten
    yoghurt, salt, and cream. Simmer till the oil
    separates from the curry. Strain the curry
    and infuse fenugreek leaves.
2. **For the cottage cheese rolls**, heat the
    oil in a pan; fry the cumin seeds, onions,
    tomatoes, ginger, and green chillies. Add
    turmeric powder, mashed cottage cheese,
    salt, and green coriander.
3. Line the cottage cheese sheets with
    cooked cottage cheese and roll into
    cylinders. Cut the cylinders into two and tie
    into log bundles with the help of scallions.
    Make four log bundles.
4. Present the log bundles standing vertically
    on fenugreek curry.

Paneer Tukra in Potato Baskets

Cottage cheese in potato baskets

INGREDIENTS

For the marinade
40 Cottage cheese (*malai paneer*), cut into 1.5"
   cubes
Salt to taste
2 Juice of lemons (*nimbu*)
1 cup / 200 gm / 7 oz Gram flour (*besan*)
1 tbsp / 15 gm Refined flour (*maida*)
1 tsp / 5 gm Red chilli powder
1 Egg
1 tbsp / 15 gm Red chilli paste
1 tsp / 5 gm Ginger-garlic (*adrak-lasan*) paste
½ tsp / 2½ gm Bishop's weed (*ajwain*)
Vegetable oil for frying

For the tempering
1 tbsp / 15 ml Vegetable oil
2 pods Garlic, chopped
1 tbsp / 15 gm Green chillies, chopped
1 tbsp / 15 gm Ginger, chopped
1 Green pepper (*Shimla mirch*), diced into 1.5"
   pieces
1 Red pepper, diced into 1.5" pieces
1 Yellow pepper, diced into 1.5" pieces
1 Tomato, diced into 1.5" pieces
1 Onion, diced into 1.5" pieces
1 tsp / 5 gm Cumin (*jeera*) powder
1 tsp / 5 gm *Chaat masala*
1 Juice of lemon (*nimbu*)
½ cup / 100 gm / 3½ oz Green coriander (*hara
   dhaniya*), chopped
4 Potato baskets for presentation (see p. 41)

METHOD

1. **For the marinade**, mix the cottage cheese with salt, lemon juice, gram flour, refined flour, red chilli powder, egg, red chilli paste, ginger-garlic paste, and Bishop's weed.
2. Lightly fry the cottage cheese cubes in hot oil till golden brown.
3. **For the tempering**, heat the oil in a pan; add garlic and fry. Add green chillies and ginger.
4. To the above, add the cubed green, red, and yellow pepper along with tomato, and onion.
5. Now add the pre-fried cottage cheese cubes. Season with cumin powder and *chaat masala*.
6. Toss everything together. Sprinkle lemon juice and garnish with green coriander.
7. Serve in potato baskets.

Subz Galouti

Smoked vegetarian kebabs

INGREDIENTS

For the kebabs
1 Carrot (*gajar*)
½ cup / 100 gm / 3½ oz Green peas (*hara mutter*)
½ cup / 100 gm / 3½ oz Cauliflower (*phool gobhi*), cleaned, cut into florets
1 Potato, medium-sized
½ cup / 100 gm / 3½ oz Corn, yellow, fresh kernels
4"-long Lotus stems (*kamal kakri*), peeled, cleaned
8 Mushrooms, button
1 Yam (*jimikand*), small
½ cup / 100 gm / 3½ oz Roasted Bengal gram (*chana dal*) powder
1 tbsp / 15 gm Ginger-garlic (*adrak-lasan*) paste
¼ cup / 50 gm / 1¾ oz Golden fried onions, crushed
¼ cup / 50 gm / 1¾ oz Cashew nut (*kaju*) paste
1 gm Saffron (*kesar*), soaked in warm water
Salt to taste
1 tsp / 5 gm *Galouti masala*
a few drops Screwpine water (*kewda*)
1 tsp / 5 gm *Garam masala* powder

For smoking
2 Live coal
a pinch Clove (*laung*) powder
1 tsp / 5 gm Ghee

For the accompaniment
4 *Rumali paratha*
2 Onion rings
4 Lemons (*nimbu*), cut into wedges

METHOD

1. Boil carrot, green peas, cauliflower, potato, corn, lotus stem, mushrooms and yam. Blend to a fine paste.
2. To the blended vegetables, mix in Bengal gram flour, ginger-garlic paste, crushed onions, cashew nut paste, saffron, salt, *galouti masala*, screwpine water, and *garam masala* powder.
3. Rub in the above ingredients and smoke with ghee and clove powder to impart flavour.
4. Make small patties with wet palm and pan-fry in moderately hot oil. Remove with a slotted spoon and drain the excess oil on absorbent paper towels.
5. Serve hot with *rumali paratha*, onion rings and lemon wedges.

Palak Patta Chaat

Deep-fried spinach served with tamarind chutney

INGREDIENTS

4 cups / 1.5 kg / 3.3 lb Spinach (*palak*) leaves,
  shredded
Salt to taste
¾ cup / 150 gm / 5 oz Gram flour (*besan*)
¼ cup / 50 gm / 1¾ oz Refined flour (*maida*)
1 tsp / 5 gm Ginger (*adrak*), chopped
1 tsp / 5 gm Green chilli, chopped
¼ tsp Bishop's weeds (*ajwain*)
½ tsp / 2½ gm Cumin (*jeera*) seeds, crushed
Vegetable oil for frying

For the accompaniment
½ cup / 100 gm / 3½ oz Tamarind (*imli*) chutney

METHOD

1. Apply salt to the spinach and rest for 10
    minutes. Squeeze the spinach and mix in
    the remaining ingredients.
2. Deep-fry the spinach in moderately hot oil.
    Remove with a slotted spoon and drain the
    excess oil on absorbent paper towels.
3. Serve hot and crisp with tamarind chutney.

Moong Dal Palak

Green gram cooked with spinach

INGREDIENTS

For the green gram
1 cup / 200 gm / 7 oz Green gram (*moong dal*)
Salt to taste
2 Bay leaves (*tej patta*)
½ tsp / 2½ gm Turmeric (*haldi*) powder

For the tempering
2 tbsp / 30 gm / 1 oz Ghee
¼ tsp Cumin (*jeera*) seeds
4 Dry red chillies (*sookhi lal mirch*)
½ tsp / 2½ gm Garlic (*lasan*), chopped
3 tbsp / 45 gm / 1½ oz Onions, chopped
½ tsp / 2½ gm Green chillies, chopped
1 tsp / 5 gm Ginger (*adrak*), chopped
½ tsp / 2½ gm Red chilli powder
2 tbsp / 30 gm / 1 oz Tomatoes, chopped
2 cups / 500 gm / 1.1 lb Spinach (*palak*) leaves,
   shredded
1 tbsp / 15 gm Butter
1 tsp / 5 gm Green coriander (*hara dhaniya*),
   chopped

METHOD

1   Wash the dal under running water and boil
    with salt, bay leaves, and turmeric powder.
    Simmer the dal till it gets cooked and
    thickens.
2. **For the tempering**, heat the ghee in a pan;
    fry cumin seeds, dry red chillies, garlic,
    onions, green chillies, ginger and red chilli
    powder.
3. Add tomatoes and spinach leaves to the
    tempering. Cook the spinach leaves and
    tomatoes for 3-4 minutes.
4. Add the tempering to the cooked dal and
    simmer for around 5 minutes.
5. Serve hot topped with butter and green
    coriander.

rice

Murg Paraat Pulao

Chicken mixed with flavoured rice

INGREDIENTS

For the chicken
500 gm / 1.1 lb Chicken boneless cubes (*tikka*)
¼ cup / 50 ml / 1¾ fl oz Vegetable oil
½ tsp / 2½ gm Cumin (*jeera*) seeds
4 Green cardamoms (*choti elaichi*)
1 Cinnamon (*dalchini*) stick
2 Bay leaves (*tej patta*)
2 cups / 400 gm / Onions, chopped
1 tbsp / 15 gm Ginger-garlic (*adrak-lasan*)
  paste
1 tsp / 5 gm Red chilli powder
2 tsp / 10 gm Coriander (*dhaniya*) powder
½ cup / 100 gm / 3½ oz Tomatoes, chopped
2 tbsp / 30 gm / 1 oz Cashew nut (*kaju*) paste
Salt to taste
¼ tsp *Garam masala* powder
1 tbsp / 15 gm Green coriander (*hara dhaniya*),
  chopped

For the pulao
2 tbsp / 30 ml / 1 fl oz Vegetable oil
1 Cinnamon stick
6 Cloves (*laung*)
1 Bay leaf
2 Black cardamoms (*badi elaichi*)
½ tsp / 2½ gm Cumin seeds
2 cups / 400 gm Basmati rice, soaked for 30
  minutes
Salt to taste

For the finishing
1 tsp / 5 ml Vegetable oil
1 tbsp / 15 gm Ginger, juliennes
1 Green chilli, slit
1 tbsp / 15 gm Onion, fried till golden
1 tsp / 5 gm *Meat masala*

METHOD

1. **For the chicken**, heat the oil and fry cumin seeds, green cardamoms, cinnamon stick, and bay leaves. Add onions, ginger-garlic paste, red chilli powder, coriander powder, tomatoes, and cashew paste. Add chicken and cook on low heat. Add salt and simmer till the chicken gets cooked.

2. Sprinkle *garam masala* powder and green coriander.

3. **For the pulao**, heat the oil and fry cinnamon stick, cloves, bay leaf, black cardamoms, and cumin seeds. Add rice, salt, and enough boiling water to cook the rice in a covered pan. Rest aside.

4. **For the finishing**, heat the oil; fry ginger, green chilli, and fried onions. Add chicken, rice and *meat masala*. Mix well and serve hot.

Chilgoza Pulao

Pine nut pilaf

INGREDIENTS

2 cups / 400 gm / 14 oz Basmati rice, soaked
 for 30 minutes
1 cup / 200 gm / 7 oz Pine nuts (*chilgoza*)
¼ cup / 50 ml / 1¾ fl oz Vegetable oil
2 Cinnamon (*dalchini*) sticks
8 Cloves (*laung*)
2 Bay leaves (*tej patta*)
8 Green cardamoms (*choti elaichi*)
1 tsp / 5 gm Cumin (*jeera*) seeds
½ cup / 100 gm / 3½ oz Onions, sliced
1 tbsp / 15 gm Ginger (*adrak*), juliennes
2 Green chillies, slit
Salt to taste

METHOD

1. Heat the oil in a pan; fry cinnamon sticks,
    cloves, bay leaves, green cardamoms,
    and cumin seeds. Add pine nuts, onions,
    ginger, and green chillies.
2. Add rice, salt and enough boiling hot
    water to cook the rice on low heat in a
    covered pan.
3. Serve hot garnished with pine nuts.

Chole Pulao

Rice made with chickpeas

INGREDIENTS

2 cups / 400 gm / 14 oz Basmati rice, soaked
   for 30 minutes
2 cups / 400 gm / 14 oz Chickpeas (*kabuli
   chana*), boiled, with stock
¼ cup / 50 ml / 1 ¾ fl oz Vegetable oil
2 Cinnamon (*dalchini*) sticks
8 Cloves (*laung*)
2 Bay leaves (*tej patta*)
8 Green cardamoms (*choti elaichi*)
1 tsp / 5 gm Cumin (*jeera*) seeds
½ cup / 100 gm / 3½ oz Onions, sliced
1 cup / 200 gm / 7 oz Mint (*pudina*) leaves,
   chopped
1 tbsp / 15 gm Ginger (*adrak*), juliennes
2 Green chillies, slit
Salt to taste

METHOD

1. Heat the oil in a pan; fry cinnamon sticks,
   cloves, bay leaves, green cardamoms, and
   cumin seeds. Add chickpeas, onions, mint,
   ginger, and green chillies.
2. Add rice, salt, chickpea stock, and enough
   boiling hot water to cook the rice on low
   heat in a covered pan.
3. Serve hot.

123

Mutton Pulao

Lamb curry mixed with rice

INGREDIENTS

For the lamb curry
24 Lamb, cut into curry pieces
¼ cup / 50 ml / 1¾ fl oz Vegetable oil
½ tsp / 2½ gm Cumin (*jeera*) seeds
4 Green cardamoms (*choti elaichi*)
1 Cinnamon (*dalchini*) stick
2 Bay leaves (*tej patta*)
2 cups / 400 gm / 14 oz Onions, chopped
1 tbsp / 15 gm Ginger-garlic (*adrak-lasan*)
  paste
1 tsp / 5 gm Red chilli powder
2 tsp / 10 gm Coriander (*dhaniya*) powder
½ cup / 100 gm / 3½ oz Tomatoes, chopped
Salt to taste
½ tsp / 2½ gm *Garam masala* powder
1 tbsp / 15 gm Green coriander (*hara dhaniya*),
  chopped

For the pulao
2 cups / 400 gm / 14 oz Basmati rice, soaked
  for 30 minutes
2 tbsp / 30 ml / 1 fl oz Vegetable oil
1 Cinnamon stick
6 Cloves (*laung*)
1 Bay leaf
2 Black cardamoms (*badi elaichi*)
½ tsp / 2½ gm Cumin seeds
Salt to taste

For the finishing
1 tsp / 5 ml Vegetable oil
1 tbsp / 15 gm Ginger, juliennes
1 Green chilli, slit
1 tbsp / 15 gm Onion, fried till golden
1 tsp / 5 gm *Meat masala*

METHOD

1. **For the lamb curry**, heat the oil and fry cumin seeds, green cardamoms, cinnamon stick, and bay leaves. Add onions, ginger-garlic paste, red chilli powder, coriander powder, and tomatoes. Add lamb and cook on low heat. Add 1 cup water and salt; simmer till the lamb gets cooked.
2. Sprinkle *garam masasla* powder and green coriander.
3. **For the pulao**, heat the oil and fry cinnamon stick, cloves, bay leaf, black cardamoms, and cumin seeds. Add rice, salt and enough boiling water to cook the rice in a covered pan. Rest aside.
4. **For the finishing**, heat the oil and fry ginger, green chilli, and fried onions. Add lamb curry, rice, and *meat masala*. Mix well and serve hot.

desserts

Anjeer ke Shahi Tukre

Baked figs on fried bread roundels

INGREDIENTS

10 Figs (*anjeer*), fresh
4 Bread slices
1 cup / 200 gm / 7 oz Ghee
1 cup / 200 gm / 7 oz Reduced milk (*rabdi*)
½ cup / 100 gm / 3½ oz Sugar
2 tbsp / 30 gm / 1 oz Demerara sugar
4 Silver leaves (*varq*)
4 sprigs Mint (*pudina*)
1 tbsp / 15 gm Almonds (*badam*), slivered
1 tbsp / 15 gm Pistachios (*pista*), slivered
½ cup / 100 gm / 3½ oz Mango (*aam*) pulp
¼ cup / 100 gm / 3½ oz Strawberry pulp

METHOD

1. Cut the slices of bread into roundels (4")
   and fry them in ghee
2. Soak the bread roundels in reduced milk
   mixed with sugar. Remove and place them
   in a baking tin.
3. Arrange slices of figs on top of the bread.
   Sprinkle demerara sugar and bake.
4. Transfer into a serving plate and garnish
   with silver leaves, a dollop of cream,
   mint sprigs, almond and pistachio slivers.
   Decorate the plate with mango and
   strawberry coulis

Masala Chai Kulfi

Masala tea ice cream in brandy schnapp cups

INGREDIENTS

For the kulfi
10 cups / 2 lt / 64 fl oz Milk, full-cream
¾ cup / 150 gm / 5 oz Sugar
1 tsp / 5 gm Tea masala powder
½ tsp / 2½ gm Green cardamom (*choti elaichi*)
  powder
1 tbsp / 15 gm Pistachios (*pista*), slivered,
  peeled
1 tbsp / 15 gm Almonds (*badam*), slivered
½ tbsp / 7½ gm Stabilizer

For the presentation
4 Brandy Schnapp cups (Pepper and fennel
  seeds)
Fruits for presentation (as required)
Fruit coulis (as required)

METHOD

1. **For the kulfi**, bring the milk to the boil and then simmer to reduce the milk to ¼th the quantity.
2. Add the sugar, tea masala powder, and green cardamom powder to the mixture. Remove and cool keep aside to cool.
3. Fold in pistachios, almonds, and stabilizer to the mix. Churn the mixture to freeze and store at 15°C / 60°F.
4. **For presentation**, serve the *masala chai kulfi* scooped in brandy schnapp cups along with cut fruits and fruit coulis.

Strawberry ke Shahi Tukre

Bread roundels topped with strawberries in thickened milk

INGREDIENTS

12 Strawberries, thinly sliced
2 Bread slices
1 cup / 200 gm / 7 oz Ghee
1 cup / 200 gm / 7 oz Reduced milk (*rabdi*)
½ cup / 100 gm / 3½ oz Sugar
4 Silver leaves (*varq*)
4 Mint (*pudina*) sprigs
1 tbsp / 15 gm Almond (*badam*) slivers
1 tbsp / 15 gm Pistachio (*pista*) slivers
½ cup / 100 gm / 3½ oz Mango coulis
½ cup / 100 gm / 3½ oz Raspberry coulis

METHOD

1. Cut the bread into roundels (4") and fry them in ghee.
2. Soak the fried bread in the reduced milk mixed with sugar. Remove and place them on a serving plate.
3. Arrange slices of strawberry on the bread.
4. Garnish with silver leaves, mint sprigs, almond and pistachio slivers.
5. Present as shown in the picture with mango and raspberry coulis.

Sugarcane Sorbet

Frozen sugarcane delight

INGREDIENTS

4 cups / 800 ml / 28 fl oz Sugarcane juice
6 Mint (*pudina*) leaves
1 tbsp / 15 ml Ginger (*adrak*) juice
¼ tsp Black salt (*kala namak*)
½ cup / 100 gm / 3½ oz Sugar
1 tsp / 5 ml Lemon (*nimbu*) juice
¼ tsp Cumin (*jeera*) powder
¼ tsp Stabilizer

For the presentation
4 Sorbet kettle
1 cup / 200 gm / 7 oz Dry ice
4 Sugarcane candies
4 Mint sprigs

METHOD

1. Infuse sugarcane juice with mint leaves to impart flavour. Mix in the remaining ingredients and churn in a sorbet machine.
2. Serve sorbet stuffed with sugarcane candies, garnished with mint and scooped in a kettle with dry ice smoke effect.

The Peak

Piped meringues on frozen bombes served with berries

INGREDIENTS

For the bombe
2 cups / 400 gm / 14 oz Reduced milk (*thin rabri*)
¼ cup / 50 gm / 1¾ oz Sugar
¼ tsp Cardamom (*elaichi*) powder
2 (8" x 8 ") Sponge sheets
4 *Rasgulla* mini (available in Indian sweetmeat stores)
4 *Gulab jamun* mini (available in Indian sweetmeat stores)
12 pieces Mangoes (*aam*), diced

For the meringue
1 cup / 200 gm / 7 oz Castor sugar
100 gm / 3½ oz Egg whites
½ stick Vanilla beans

For the presentation
4 Raspberries
8 Blueberries
4 Blackberries
4 bunch Red currants
¼ cup Passion fruit coulis
¼ cup Strawberry coulis

METHOD

1. **For the kulfi bombe**, mix the sugar and cardamom powder with the reduced milk and churn in an ice cream machine to make *kulfi*.
2. Line the semi-sphere bombe moulds with sponge sheet and fill in with soft *kulfi* along with diced mangoes, mini *gulab jamuns* and *rasgullas*.
3. Freeze the bombes at -18°C for a minimum of 12 hours.
4. **For the meringue**, whip the sugar and egg whites to a stiff meringue.
5. Pipe the meringue on to the bombes and re freeze it.
6. Serve torched / flambéed on the meringue along with the berries and coulis.

Khaas Malpoi

Crepe and carrot rolls on a bed of thickened milk

INGREDIENTS

For the crepes
1 cup / 200 gm / 3½ oz Refined flour (*maida*)
½ cup / 100 ml / 3½ fl oz Milk
a few strands Saffron (*kesar*), roasted, soaked
¼ cup / 50 gm / 1¾ oz Sugar
2 tbsp / 30 ml / 1 fl oz Vegetable oil

For the carrot halwa
3 cups / 600 gm / 22 oz Carrots (*gajar*), grated
1 cup / 200 ml / 7 fl oz Milk
2 tbsp / 30 gm / 1 oz Ghee
2 Green cardamoms (*choti elaichi*)
¼ cup / 50 gm / 1¾ oz Sugar
2 tbsp / 30 gm / 1 oz Dry condensed milk
2 tbsp / 30 gm / 1 oz Fresh curdled milk
  (*chenna*)
2 tbsp / 30 gm / 1 oz Powdered sugar

For the presentation
¾ cup / 150 ml / 5 fl oz Reduced milk (*sweet rabri*)
1 tsp / 5 gm Pistachio (*pista*) slivers
8 Rose petals (*gulab pankhuri*)

METHOD

1. **For the crepes,** mix flour, milk, saffron and sugar together. Make thin sweet crepes by frying small portions of batter in oil.
2. **For the carrot halwa**, simmer the carrots in milk till the milk is completely absorbed.
3. Heat the ghee in a pan and fry the green cardamoms. Add the boiled carrot and sugar. Mix in the dry condensed milk. Remove and keep aside to cool.
4. Add powdered sugar to the fresh curdled milk and cream it to a smooth texture.
5. **For the crepe and carrot rolls**, make crepe and carrot halwa rolls with sweet curdled milk piped in the centre. Wrap the rolls tightly and chill.
6. **For the presentation,** cut 1"-thick slices of carrot rolls and serve them hot on a bed of reduced milk. Garnish with rose petals and pistachio slivers.

Gulab Jamun Brulee

Caramalized Indian sweetmeat brulee

INGREDIENTS

2 cups / 400 ml / 14 fl oz Cream (60% fat)
6 Egg yolks
¼ cup / 50 gm / 1¾ oz Sugar
½ cup / 100 ml / 3 ½ fl oz Milk
4 *Gulab jamuns* (available in Indian sweetmeat
   stores)

METHOD

1. Heat the cream to approximately 80°C /
   175°F.
2. In a bowl, whisk the egg yolks and sugar till
   the sugar dissolves completely.
3. Slowly pour the cream and milk into the
   yolks, stirring constantly. Cook the mixture
   over a double boiler till it thickens.
4. Slice the gulab jamuns and spread them
   in the brulee mould. Pour the cream mix
   into the mould and transfer the mould into
   a baking tray half filled with water. Bake at
   150°C / 300°F for 45 minutes.
5. Remove after baking and keep aside to
   cool. Finish the brulee with caramelized
   castor sugar and serve.

Suggested Menus

MENU 2
For a casual brunch

Lemon Grass Rasam
(Lemon grass flavoured tomato soup)
see p. 27

Bhatti ka Jheenga
(Chargrilled prawns) see p. 34

Dum ki Nalli
(Lamb shanks served with spicy baked
potatoes) see p. 80

Chilgoza Falli
(Haricot beans cooked with pine nuts
and cherry tomatoes) see p. 94

Moong Dal Palak
(Green gram cooked with spinach)
see p. 117

Anjeer ke Shahi Tukre
(Baked figs on fried bread) see p. 129

MENU 1
For an elegant dinner party

Bhune Makai ka Shorba
(Roasted corn soup) see p. 23

Crab Varqui
(Layered crabs served with prawns)
see p. 38

Subz Galouti
(Smoked vegetarian kebabs)
see p. 115

Murg Khatta Pyaz
(Chicken kebabs in tomato gravy)
see p. 69

Indian Breads

The Peak
(Piped meringues on frozen bombes
served with berries) see p. 136

MENU 4

For a vegetarian feast

Palak Patta Chaat
(Deep-fried spinach served with
tamarind chutney) see p. 116

Khumb Varqui
(Mushrooms in tomato gravy layered
with phyllo sheets) see p. 100

Dilli ki Challi
(Spiced corn on cob) see p. 105

Paneer Parcha
(Cottage cheese rolls in white fenugreek
gravy) see p. 110

Chilgoza Pulao
(Pine nut pilaf) see p. 122

Gulab Jamun Brulee
(Caramalized Indian sweet meat brulee)
see p. 141

MENU 3

For a romantic repast

Hare Chane ka Shorba
(Green gram soup) see p. 24

Tandoori Pink Salmon
(Chargrilled Salmon served with lemon)
see p. 59

Gucchi Khumb
(Mushrooms in tomato gravy) see p. 98

Lal Mirch ka Paneer
(Skewered cottage cheese garnished
with red chillies) see p. 103

Murg Paraat Pulao
(Chicken mixed with flavoured rice)
see p. 120

Khaas Malpoi
(Crepe and carrot rolls on a bed of
thickened milk) see p. 138

Suggested Wine Pairing:

MENU 1: Try a fruity white wine to reflect the acidic flavours, such as a Reisling or Sauvignon blanc

MENU 2: A medium red will offset the richness of the food nicely, try a Merlot

MENU 3: Keep it light with Champagne or Pinot Noir

MENU 4: Best enjoyed with a glass of Brunello di Montalcino or Cabernet Sauvignon

Glossary
of Food & Cooking Terms

Baste: Moisten the meat, poultry or game with oil or butter during roasting.

Batter: A mixture of flour, liquid and sometimes other ingredients of a thin, creamy consistency.

Blend: To mix together thoroughly two or more ingredients.

Broil: Dry roast the food items in a heavy-bottomed pan on low heat without using oil or water.

Chargrill: To grill food especially meat over a fire of charcoal or wood.

Coat: To cover food that is to be fried with flour, egg, and breadcrumbs or batter.

Coulis: A purée of fruit or vegetables, used as a sauce or flavouring agent to other sauces or soups. As sauces, they are thinned down just enough to reach the proper consistency, but not so much as to alter the intense flavour of the purée.

Curdle: To separate milk into curd and whey by acid or excessive heat.

Garnish: An edible decoration added to a savoury or sweet dish to improve its appearance.

Grind: To reduce hard food such as pulses, lentils, rice, and so forth, to fine or coarse paste in a grinder or blender.

Julienne: Garnished with fine strips of cooked or raw vegetables.

Knead: To work a dough by hand or machine until smooth.

Marinade: A seasoned mixture of oil, vinegar, lemon juice, and so forth, in which meat, poultry or fish is left for some time to soften and add flavour to it.

Mille-Feuille: Small rectangular pastries made of crisp layers of puff pastry and pastry cream. This may also include savoury fillings of similar presentation. The word mille-feuille means a thousand leaves.

Purée: To press food through a fine sieve or blend it in a blender or food processor to a smooth, thick mixture.

Sauté: To cook in an open pan in hot, shallow fat, tossing the food to prevent it from sticking.

Sear: To brown meat or fish quickly over very high heat either in a frying pan, under a broiler or in a hot oven. Searing seals in the food's juices and provides a crisp tasty exterior.

Seasoning: Salt, pepper, spices, herbs, and so forth, added to give depth of flavour.

Simmer: To boil gently on low heat.

Skewer: Fasten together pieces of food compactly on a specially designed long pin, for cooking.

Smoking: The process of imparting a smoked flavour to the preparation. Heat a piece of coal over the flame till it becomes red hot. Overlap 2-3 onion peels to form a small cup. Place it in the middle of the dish, with the preparation to be smoked. Place the coal in the onion-peel cup. Smoke with either of the following:

Steam: To cook food on a rack or in steamer basket over a boiling liquid in a covered pan. Steaming retains flavour, shape, texture, and nutrients better than boiling or poaching.

Stir: To mix with a circular action, usually with a spoon, fork or spatula.

Syrup: A concentrated solution of sugar in water.

Tandoor: Tandoor is a large coal-fired oven. It is easily adaptable to the oven, the electrical grill or the microwave. Tandoor is akin to the western barbecue, but with more delicate flavours and with marinades which enhance the flavour of the principle ingredient.

Temper: To fry spices and flavourings in hot oil or ghee, and to pour this over the main preparation.